Class no. 942·062
SMI
Acc. no. 28790

KU-071-689

# Oliver Cromwell

**Politics and Religion in the
English Revolution,
1640-1658**

Ridge Danyers : Marple Site

\* M 0 0 2 8 7 9 0 \*

# Oliver Cromwell

## Politics and Religion in the English Revolution, 1640-1658

David L. Smith

*Fellow of Selwyn College,*
*Cambridge*

RIDGE DANYERS COLLEGE
MARPLE CAMPUS LIBRARY
HIBBERT LANE, MARPLE
STOCKPORT SK6 7PA
Tel. 0161 484 6625

CAMBRIDGE
UNIVERSITY PRESS

PUBLISHED BY THE PRESS SYNDICATE OF THE UNIVERSITY OF CAMBRIDGE
The Pitt Building, Trumpington Street, Cambridge, United Kingdom

CAMBRIDGE UNIVERSITY PRESS
The Edinburgh Building, Cambridge CB2 2RU, UK      http://www.cup.cam.ac.uk
40 West 20th Street, New York, NY 10011–4211, USA   http://www.cup.org
10 Stamford Road, Oakleigh, Melbourne 3166, Australia
Ruiz de Alarcón 13, 28014 Madrid, Spain

© Cambridge University Press

First published 1991
Reprinted 1992, 1999

Printed in the United Kingdom at the University Press, Cambridge

*British Library Cataloguing in Publication data*
Smith, David L.
  Oliver Cromwell: politics and religion in the English
  Revolution, 1640–1658. – (Cambridge topics in history)
  1. England. Cromwell, Oliver
  I. Title
  942.064092

ISBN 0 521 38896 1

*H J, Apr '01*
*M 329.062*
*942.*
*28790*

NOTICE TO TEACHERS
It is illegal to reproduce any part of this work in material form
(including photocopying and electronic storage) except under the
following circumstances:
(i) where you are abiding by a licence granted to your school or
institution by the Copyright Licensing Agency;
(ii) where no such licence exists, or where you wish to exceed the
terms of the licence, and you have gained the written permission of
Cambridge University Press;
(iii) where you are allowed to reproduce without permission under
the provision of Chapter 3 of the Copyright, Designs and Patents
Act 1988.

SE

# Contents

For my Mother and Father

# Acknowledgements

I wish to thank John Morrill for his invaluable assistance, encouragement and support throughout the preparation of this book. I am also very grateful for the helpful advice of Stephanie Boyd at Cambridge University Press. I am indebted to Ian Atherton for sending me a transcription of document 1.15.

The author and publisher are grateful to the following for permission to reproduce extracts and illustrations:

2.12 L. Miller, *John Milton and the Oldenburg Safeguard* (Loewenthal Press, New York, 1985); 2.14, 5.11, 5.16 *Swedish Diplomats at Cromwell's Court, 1655–6*, ed. M. Roberts (Camden Society, fourth series, vol. XXXVI, 1988); 2.20 The Ashmolean Museum, Oxford; 2.21, 2.22, 2.26 reproduced by Courtesy of the Trustees of the British Museum; 2.23 The Mansell Collection; 2.24 by permission of the British Library; 2.25 by permission of the Syndics of Cambridge University Library; 6.2 Christopher Hill, *God's Englishman* (Penguin edition, Harmondsworth, 1972), reproduced by permission of George Weidenfeld & Nicolson Limited and Penguin Books USA Inc.; 6.3 Derek Hirst, *Authority and Conflict: England, 1603–1658* (Edward Arnold, London, 1986); 6.4 J.P. Kenyon, *Stuart England* (2nd edition, Penguin, Harmondsworth, 1985), copyright © J.P. Kenyon, 1978, 1985, reproduced by permission of Penguin Books Ltd; 6.5 Blair Worden, *The Rump Parliament, 1648–1653* (Cambridge University Press, 1974); 6.6 Austin Woolrych, *Commonwealth to Protectorate* (Oxford University Press, 1982); 6.7 H.R. Trevor-Roper, *Religion, the Reformation and Social Change* (Macmillan, London, 1967); 6.8 Robert S. Paul, *The Lord Protector* (Lutterworth Press, London, 1955); 6.10 John Morrill, 'Cromwell and his Contemporaries', in *Oliver Cromwell and the English Revolution*, ed. John Morrill (Longman, Harlow, 1990).

*Cover illustration:* Oliver Cromwell by Robert Walker, *c.* 1649; reproduced by permission of the National Portrait Gallery.

# Introduction

## A   The problem

By any criterion, the events which gripped mid-seventeenth-century England were remarkable. For the first time since the Wars of the Roses in the fifteenth century, the English nation was torn in two by civil war. But whereas some medieval monarchs had been deposed, in 1649 the King was unprecedentedly put on trial and publicly executed. The monarchy was then abolished outright. The republican government which replaced it for eleven years (1649–60) is unique in English history. Their very strangeness gives the events of the English Revolution a compelling claim to be studied. In the past, some scholars have advanced even grander claims. In the nineteenth and early twentieth centuries, the so-called 'Whig' historians argued that the developments of the 1640s and 1650s were crucial in England's historic progress away from royal absolutism and towards constitutional monarchy. In the mid-twentieth century, 'Marxist' historians suggested that the same developments encouraged the growth of capitalism in England. Such interpretations are no longer fashionable, but the events themselves remain just as dramatic, colourful and bizarre. Even if their causes and long-term significance are subjects of intense debate, the Civil Wars and Interregnum were without doubt a time of unparalleled (and wholly unexpected) turmoil and upheaval. Few periods in the history of any country are so intriguing yet so difficult to explain.

These qualities of dynamism, savagery and elusiveness are also apparent in the figure who dominated the English Revolution: Oliver Cromwell. Within barely fifteen years, this obscure provincial farmer emerged as one of the most successful military leaders of his time, and subsequently became Head of State and Lord Protector of England, Scotland and Ireland. During the 1650s he wielded the most extensive powers ever possessed by an English ruler. More than any other individual, he was responsible for the King's defeat in the Civil Wars. Yet he himself was later offered the Crown, and only declined it after long and anguished hesitation. This is just one of numerous paradoxes in Cromwell's extraordinary career. There are few historical figures whose name conjures up so many diverse and seemingly contradictory images. Are we to see Cromwell as a soldier or a statesman; as a man of consistent ideals or a self-seeking opportunist; as a conservative country squire or a revolutionary zealot; as a bigoted tyrant or a champion of civil and religious liberty; as a sincere and godly man or a canting hypocrite? Precisely how great was his influence over events? Did he leave an enduring legacy or did his achievements die with him? As we shall see throughout this book, such questions have divided Cromwell's contemporaries and later historians alike. The documents and commentary should help you to formulate answers of your own.

The purpose of this introduction is briefly to review the main areas of debate over Cromwell's career (Section B), and then to explain the lay-out of the book (Section C). This chapter, like the others, assumes that you already have an outline knowledge of Cromwell's career and some sense of the course of British history during the 1640s and 1650s. These may be gained by reading any of the surveys or biographies listed in the Bibliography on pp. 113–17.

## B    Areas of debate

It is possible to isolate five aspects of Cromwell's career which have proved especially controversial: his motives; his aims; the extent to which he was sincere; the methods which he used; and the nature of his impact on England. This section will examine each of these debates in turn.

### I    Motives

Any person who rises from rural obscurity to dominate their world must surely possess immense drive and dynamism. Yet what exactly spurred Cromwell on, what made him fight for Parliament in the 1640s and rule England in the 1650s, has never been agreed. What motivated him? What stimulated the almost manic energy and urgency noted by Cromwell's contemporaries?

Two sharply contrasting answers have been advanced. The first is that Cromwell's motives were essentially *ideological*. He was a man of firm convictions who pursued consistent principles throughout his career. These ideals have been hotly debated: you will find them described variously as a wish to make England a freer and more egalitarian society [6.2]; a hatred of royal tyranny; and (most commonly) a desire to conform to the will of God and to draw the English people into more godly ways [6.8–6.10]. (Boldface numbers in square brackets refer to the documents in Chapters 1–6.) Nevertheless, all these arguments share the same belief that Cromwell was driven on, as a soldier and as a statesman, by ideological principles. His pragmatic approach to outward forms, both constitutional [2.1] and religious [3.12], did not preclude a constant and selfless commitment to broader ideals. Though not 'wedded and glued to *forms* of government' [2.1], Cromwell was 'wedded and glued' to the *ends* of government. It was his vision of those ends which guided his actions.

But there is also a second, very different, interpretation of Cromwell's motives. This presents him not as a man of principle but as a self-seeking opportunist, a person driven by ruthless ambition and lust for power. According to this view, Cromwell was prepared to abandon friends, institutions and ideals in order to enhance his own power. Time and again, he would adopt a proposal and then discard it, leaving its proponents feeling deeply betrayed. These 'undefended inconsistencies' [6.7] led many of Cromwell's contemporaries to attack him as selfish and Machiavellian. Later, we will look at the grievances of the Leveller leader John Lilburne in 1649 [4.18]; the defenders of the Rump Parliament [2.9]; committed republicans [1.16; 2.17; 4.20; 5.26]; and many others [2.18–2.19; 3.20–3.23; 4.17–4.19; 5.25; 5.27]. Such views have been echoed by some later historians [6.4].

This controversy shows no signs of being resolved. Supporters of the first interpretation can argue that it makes more sense of Cromwell's own words, and that his broader ideological goals account for his apparent inconsistencies. Furthermore, some episodes are extremely difficult to explain in terms of Cromwell's ambition. Why, when he possessed absolute power in the summer of 1653 did he choose to surrender it to Barebone's Parliament [3.6; 4.8]? However, it could be argued that this was the exception which proved the rule; that Cromwell's other political manoeuvres nearly always left his own dominance intact. Because he always retained the army's support, and because the office of Lord Protector was not limited by existing laws, Cromwell wielded more raw power during the 1650s than any other English ruler. It is therefore extremely difficult to *prove* that he was not motivated by self-interest. His refusal of the kingship may have been for reasons of principle, as he himself claimed [2.16; 3.9]. Alternatively, you might agree with some well-informed contemporaries who claimed that Cromwell knew he was more powerful as Lord Protector [2.15].

It may be, however, that these arguments assume too rigid a distinction between ideology and interest. If Cromwell believed that he was God's agent, with a divinely appointed mission, he would naturally tend to see any resistance to himself as resistance to God's will. It was therefore his *duty* to God to remain in control. Might Cromwell have coveted power for himself precisely *because* he was a man of principle? If so, it may be possible to reconcile these two contrasting interpretations of his motives.

## 2  Aims

The second controversy concerns the nature of Cromwell's aims. What did he *want?* The debate here is over how far Cromwell sought radical changes in English politics, religion and society, and to what extent he always remained at heart a conservative country squire. It seems fairly clear that there were very deep tensions within Cromwell's own nature over which aspects of the status quo should be preserved. Most historians now agree that he was to some extent *both* a radical *and* a conservative, but the precise balance between these is still disputed.

The most radical dimension of Cromwell's personality was almost certainly his religion. It was here that he was least committed to the existing order. By the mid-1630s his letters show both a deep resentment of Laud's policies [3.1] and an intense personal faith [3.2]. In February 1641 he demanded the abolition of bishops [1.4]. He seems to have seen the two Civil Wars as genuinely religious experiences [3.3–3.4]. During the 1650s he expressed ideals of religious toleration which contrasted dramatically both with the earlier Anglican church and with the views of most of his contemporaries [3.10–3.14]. This vision of peaceful co-existence between autonomous sects clearly stamps Cromwell as an 'Independent' – one of the most radical religious stances in mid-seventeenth-century England. Even those historians who deny that Cromwell's faith was his sole guiding principle [6.5–6.7] would nevertheless agree that he sought far-reaching changes in England's religious order.

There is rather more controversy over the extent to which this religious radicalism spilled over into Cromwell's political and social attitudes. The debate is encouraged by the blatant paradoxes in Cromwell's career. Here was a man who led the military campaigns against Charles I and who (eventually) supported the regicide, yet who almost became king himself and always retained a deep commitment to the concept of Parliaments. One interpretation [6.5–6.6] sees a fundamental tension – or, in Blair Worden's phrase, 'ideological schizophrenia' [6.5] – between Cromwell's religious radicalism and his constitutional conservatism. He was torn between two equally strong but quite incompatible aims. Another thesis, recently advanced by Dr John Adamson (see the article cited in the Bibliography on p. 115), argues that Cromwell was committed to the Long Parliament provided that it accepted a responsibility to the godly. But when it broke this trust he did not hesitate to dissolve it. Despite their different emphases, both these interpretations acknowledge Cromwell's conservative approach to the constitution; and both have clearly moved away from some nineteenth-century images of Cromwell as a revolutionary king-killer and constitutional experimenter.

There is much less agreement over the nature of Cromwell's social aims. Two contrasting pictures have emerged. One is of a typical country squire with all the conservative prejudices and vested interests of his class: someone who not only accepted but admired the existing social hierarchy [4.2] and who strongly resisted attempts to subvert it [4.1; 4.3]. Cromwell was a social reactionary, despised by the Levellers [4.16]. The other, quite different, picture sees Cromwell as a radical social engineer, a man whose religious beliefs moulded his social attitudes. At times Cromwell attacked the hereditary nobility [1.8] and appeared to seek instead 'the rule of the saints'. His promotions in both the military and the civil spheres were apparently designed to achieve this [1.8–1.9; 4.7–4.9]. At the very least, Cromwell wanted a 'reformation of manners', a campaign of moral rearmament to turn people's hearts and minds towards the things of God [3.15–3.19].

As we will see, there is good evidence to support *both* views. It seems very likely that this debate, and the wider controversy over Cromwell's aims, reflect genuine complexities and ambivalences within his own personality. When trying to unravel what objectives Cromwell pursued, perhaps we should remember his own words: 'No one rises so high as he who knows not whither he is going.'

## 3 Sincerity

This quotation from Cromwell brings us to the third area of debate. How far should we believe what Cromwell *said*? Was he sincere or a dissembling hypocrite? This issue, which is central to our understanding of Cromwell, has been the subject of furious debate ever since he lived.

Here again we find diametrically opposed answers both in the historiography and in contemporary accounts. Many of those who knew Cromwell believed that he used high-minded rhetoric to excuse inconsistencies [3.20] and to outflank opponents [3.22]. His repeated dissolutions of Parliaments and his imprisonment of those who crossed him were accompanied by sanctimonious assertions of his own virtues and rectitude [2.17–2.19; 4.17–4.20; 6.7]. We will see that many foreign diplomats were very sceptical of Cromwell's integrity [5.18; 5.20; 5.23]. Even some observers who praised Cromwell's good *intentions* thought that power had later corrupted him [3.21; 3.23].

Such views have seemed all the more plausible in the light of a series of episodes in which Cromwell got precisely what he wanted yet denied any involvement. Most spectacularly, Cromwell insisted that he had no foreknowledge of the King's seizure from Holmby House in June 1647 [3.20]. Yet only three days earlier the officer responsible (Cornet Joyce) had visited Cromwell's home in London. In December 1648, Cromwell arrived at Westminster within hours of Pride's Purge [1.23]: he was thus able to take advantage of it without being implicated in it. Many historians (especially Dr Blair Worden) are highly suspicious of Cromwell's account of the Rump's activities just before he dissolved it [2.8]; and there is another large question-mark over whether he knew in advance about *The Humble Petition and Advice* which offered him the Crown [2.12–2.14]. These are just some of the instances in which Cromwell benefited from political developments but denied responsibility for them. Many have refused to believe that he was as innocent as he claimed.

Yet there is absolutely no evidence which *proves* that Cromwell deliberately lied on any of these occasions. This has persuaded some historians that he was sincere. For example, in his introduction to *Oliver Cromwell and the English Revolution*, Dr John Morrill writes: 'Can there be so much smoke without fire? My personal view is that in this case there can. The balance of the evidence points towards Cromwell's insouciance and impulsiveness and against a calculated cunning and deliberate, brazen hypocrisy.' Dr Morrill and others would argue that if Cromwell's words contain inconsistencies and inaccuracies, this was because he was *self-deceiving* rather than insincere. He was not a liar or a hypocrite; but he *was* capable of deluding himself about God's will and about his own motives.

In the course of this book, we will examine many of Cromwell's letters and speeches, together with attacks by his enemies. How far we should trust him – whether he unconsciously deceived himself or consciously tried to deceive others – is an issue which these documents will help you to decide for yourselves.

## 4   Methods

The fourth controversy surrounds the methods which Cromwell employed both as a soldier and as a politician. Was he a champion of liberty or an oppressive tyrant? This debate is clearly reflected in two contrasting popular images of Cromwell. The first is that celebrated each year by the Cromwell Association: it is of the man who destroyed Stuart tyranny; the promoter of civil and religious liberty; the opponent of dogma, privilege and injustice. By contrast, the second popular image depicts an autocratic tyrant, a military dictator who imprisoned his enemies at will, who gratuitously wrecked castles and churches, who butchered the Irish, and who ruled as arbitrarily as the Stuarts. This section will examine each of these images in turn.

When Cromwell died, the anonymous *Exact Character or Narrative of the*

*Late Right Noble and Magnificent Lord Oliver Cromwell* (London, 1658) praised him as one who 'constantly stood firm and trusty in upholding' the 'liberties of his country'. This verdict has been most recently echoed by Roger Howell, who described Cromwell as 'a major contributor to the growth of English liberty' (see the article cited in the Bibliography on p. 116). There is clearly evidence to support this argument. Cromwell fought to defend the rights of Parliament against Charles I [1.3; 2.7]. He was instrumental in the King's defeat and in the abolition of monarchy [1.19–1.24]. As Lord Protector he repeatedly affirmed his commitment to civil and religious liberty [2.3–2.5]; he advocated the reform of the legal system to make it less oppressive and more accessible to ordinary people [4.13–4.15]; and he was far more tolerant of religious diversity than most of his contemporaries [3.10–3.14]. The Victorian statue of Cromwell guarding the Houses of Parliament perfectly symbolises this view of him as a champion of popular liberties.

But the alternative image has an equally long history. Within Cromwell's own lifetime he was attacked as a usurper and an oppressor. Contemporary broadsheets included *A Declaration of the Freeborn People of England now in Arms against the Tyranny and Oppression of Oliver Cromwell* (London, 1655). Shortly after this appeared, Cromwell established the military rule of the Major-Generals to root out opposition and to *enforce* a 'reformation of manners' [4.5]. He claimed to rule 'for the people's good, not what pleases them' (see John Morrill's introduction to *Oliver Cromwell and the English Revolution*). If necessary, he was prepared to flout laws, to imprison without trial, and to rule according to his own will [4.16–4.20]. Dr Worden has recently suggested that even Cromwell's religious toleration had its limits; certainly 'papists' and 'prelatists' (supporters of bishops) were always excluded. Cromwell's virulent anti-Catholicism was most notoriously displayed during the conquest of Ireland in 1649–50 [3.5; 5.6; 5.9]. While always remaining technically within the rules of seventeenth-century warfare, he nevertheless showed a brutality not seen elsewhere in his career.

These two images seem incompatible, but there are perhaps two ways in which they might be reconciled. First, Cromwell may have had deeper objectives which explain what look like contradictory policies. It may be that *both* his 'tyranny' *and* his promotion of 'liberty' were designed to further other goals. Both, for example, might be related to his religious attitudes [6.8–6.10]. Another possible answer lies in the tension between Cromwell's wishes as an individual and his duties as a ruler [6.5]. He may have *preferred* to sponsor freedom and toleration, but been obliged to rule autocratically in order to preserve order [3.12; 4.6]. Cromwell saw the latter as his prime duty, and in April 1657 likened himself to 'a good constable set to keep the peace of the parish' [2.2]. Inevitably, such a public role sometimes conflicted with Cromwell's own personal instincts.

## 5   Impact

Finally, what impact did the 'good constable' have on England? In what ways did he change English government, religion and society during his own lifetime? What (if any) was his legacy? In one sense, Cromwell's impact on his times seems beyond dispute. The force of his personality, the extent of his powers, and his decisive influence on military and political developments will all become apparent throughout this book. English history during the 1640s and 1650s would have been very different had Cromwell not lived.

Yet, paradoxically, many historians now argue that Cromwell achieved much less than he wanted and that he died a bitterly disappointed man. He was unable to establish a stable or lasting regime and the English republic collapsed within two years of his death. He longed to preside over a godly commonwealth; to nurture religious conviction; to turn people towards the things of the Lord [3.15–3.17]. But he secured at best a grudging acquiescence under threat of military coercion [2.6; 3.18–3.19; 4.6]. He sought to reunite society after the bloodshed of the 1640s; yet his policy of 'healing and settling' itself brought him into conflict with Parliament [4.10–4.12]. As the 1650s progressed, there was a steady drift back towards familiar institutions in both central and local government, and there is little evidence that the traditional social dominance of the nobility and gentry was significantly reduced. Cromwell's plans for Scotland and Ireland were never fully realised [5.1–5.9]. It has also been argued that the basic assumptions of his foreign policy rapidly became obsolete when France emerged as the leading European power in the later seventeenth century [5.25–5.26]. There were thus clear limits to the longer-term impact of Cromwellian rule.

The reasons for this are much more difficult to uncover and many questions remain wide open. It is far from clear whether Cromwell failed because his *aims* were unrealistic in themselves, or because his *methods* alienated too many people, or some combination of both. Another interpretation sees Cromwell's goals as mutually contradictory. It was precisely *because* he hankered after religious zeal and refused 'to settle for settlement' that his government remained unstable and society unhealed [6.10]. The broader significance of Cromwell's failure is also contested. Should we condemn him as a stubborn nuisance who prevented a peaceful settlement and resisted the inevitable return of monarchy [6.4]? Does his limited long-term impact prove that he sought the impossible? Or should we see him as a tragic hero and admire the tenacity with which he pursued a noble vision [6.2]? Is what he attempted more important than what he achieved?

Similar debate surrounds the nature of Cromwell's legacy. Many of the 'Whig' historians believed that Cromwell anticipated a modern 'liberal' outlook in both Church and State; that he established values of parliamentary government and religious tolerance which reached their apotheosis in late-Victorian England. To S.R. Gardiner, Cromwell was 'the national hero of the nineteenth century' (see also 6.1). By contrast, more recent historians have tended to place Cromwell within the context of his own times and to stress the differences between his aspirations and modern 'liberalism'. Many have emphasised the extent to which his achievements died with him. The Restoration decisively re-established the constitutional and religious structures of pre-Civil War England. Some scholars argue that Cromwell's encouragement of religious nonconformity bore lasting fruit [6.3]; but others are more struck by how many of his values and priorities became submerged after 1660 [6.4; 6.10]. The religious pluralism and constitutional monarchy of Britain today both have very complex origins, and it is difficult to link either directly to Cromwell.

In the end, we return to the point with which we began: the intrinsic fascination of Cromwell's life and career. We may not be able to justify studying him as a man who set England on the path to modernity. But as someone who dominated his world for nearly twenty years, who wielded immense powers, and without whom events would have looked very different, he repays careful investigation. He was an extraordinary human being: as John Maidstone, the steward and cofferer of Cromwell's protectoral household, later wrote, 'a larger soul hath seldom dwelt in a house of clay'.

## C  Documents and topics

The documents and commentary in this book are designed to help you form your own opinions on these complex debates. The 130 extracts are inevitably a very small selection from the vast body of evidence bearing on Cromwell's career. Ironically, although Cromwell remains one of the most enigmatic figures in English history he is also one of the best documented. The relevant materials include Cromwell's own letters and speeches; official documents generated by the institutions of central government; contemporary newspapers and tracts; private letters, diaries and memoirs; the despatches of foreign diplomats; and original coins and engravings. Some items from each of these categories appear in this book. Throughout, my choice of sources has been governed by three aims. First, I have tried to achieve a balance between

Cromwell's *private* correspondence and his *public* utterances in speeches and declarations. You will therefore be able to assess whether he adapted his rhetoric depending on his audience. Second, I have sought a similar balance between Cromwell's own words and the accounts and depictions left by his contemporaries. This will enable you to compare Cromwell as he saw himself with Cromwell as others saw him. Finally, the documents have been chosen to illuminate the various controversies discussed above. Although they are only a selection, they should permit you to decide which arguments you find most persuasive in the light of primary evidence.

One further decision requires explanation. When quoting Cromwell's own letters and speeches, I had to choose between the two collected editions. These are *The Letters and Speeches of Oliver Cromwell, with Elucidations by Thomas Carlyle*, ed. S.C. Lomas (3 vols., London, 1904), and *The Writings and Speeches of Oliver Cromwell*, ed. W.C. Abbott (4 vols., Cambridge, Mass., 1937–47). To achieve consistency I decided to use the same edition throughout, and the former seemed preferable for several reasons. First, it is far more widely available than the Abbott edition, and this will make it much easier for you to trace the various extracts and to put them in context. Second, the texts in the Carlyle/Lomas edition are consistently superior. Abbott's edition is spoiled by many factual errors, by a failure to explain his editorial policy regarding the wide discrepancies between original sources, and by some very unreliable texts. Finally, the Carlyle/Lomas edition is very attractively laid out, and this makes it much more convenient to use. I have therefore quoted it throughout, citing it simply as 'Carlyle'.

In all extracts, I have modernised spelling and punctuation, and translated foreign documents into English. The vocabulary is as in the originals, but I have added notes to explain obscure words and phrases.

The structure of the book is as follows. The first five chapters explore Cromwell's career during the 1640s and 1650s. Chapter 1 investigates his political and military activities during the two Civil Wars. Then follow three parallel chapters devoted to Cromwell's attitudes towards, respectively, politics, religion and society. The fifth chapter examines Cromwell's relations with the rest of Britain and the wider world. Finally, Chapter 6 returns to the historiographical debates surrounding Cromwell's life. It presents ten contrasting assessments of Cromwell written by historians from the late nineteenth century to the present day. The Bibliography contains a list of books and articles in which these various topics may be taken further.

# 1 Cromwell and the Civil Wars

In 1640 Oliver Cromwell, a little-known fenland farmer, was elected to represent the city of Cambridge in the Short and Long Parliaments. Nine years later, Charles I was executed and Cromwell was the most powerful figure in England. In the intervening years of civil war, Parliament's military victories over the King owed more to Cromwell than to anyone else. This chapter examines Cromwell's career as a soldier and politician during the 1640s. How and why did he emerge from provincial obscurity to national prominence? How did he view the two sides in the Civil Wars, and they him? And why, after determined attempts to negotiate with the King, did Cromwell come to believe that he should be executed as a tyrant and traitor?

In 1640 Oliver Cromwell had few claims to fame. The Royalist Edward Hyde, later Earl of Clarendon, wrote that in the early months of the Long Parliament he was 'little taken notice of'. He was known, if at all, only for the fiery temper revealed in a dispute over the Huntingdon borough charter ten years earlier. In 1630 Cromwell launched a violent attack on the mayor and recorder of Huntingdon, condemning the new charter and those who gained power under its terms. The quarrel became so serious that the Privy Council ordered the Lord Privy Seal, the first Earl of Manchester, to investigate it: 1.1 is an extract from his report.

1.1

It pleased your lordships to refer unto me the differences in the town of Huntingdon about the renovation of their charter, and some wrongs done to Mr Mayor of Huntingdon and Mr Barnard,[I] a councillor-at-law, by disgraceful and unseemly speeches used of them by Mr Cromwell of Huntingdon . . . I have heard the said differences, and do find those supposed fears of prejudice that might be to     5
the said town, by their late altered charter . . . are causeless and ill-grounded . . .
For the words spoken of Mr Mayor and Mr Barnard by Mr Cromwell, as they were ill, so they are acknowledged to be spoken in heat and passion, and desired to be forgotten; and I find Mr Cromwell very willing to hold friendship with Mr Barnard,

who, with a good will, remitting the unkind passages past, entertained the same. So     10
I left all parties reconciled.

¹ 'Mr Barnard' = Robert Barnard, the Recorder of Huntingdon.

**Henry Montague, first Earl of Manchester and Lord Privy Seal, to the Privy Council, 6 December 1630: Public Record Office, SP 16/176/34**

But as soon as the Long Parliament assembled on 3 November 1640 Cromwell became actively involved in important and controversial issues. The next four extracts [1.2–1.5] are all taken from the fullest surviving parliamentary diary for these years, kept by the Suffolk antiquarian and future Parliamentarian Sir Simonds D'Ewes. They indicate the nature of Cromwell's political and religious concerns between late 1640 and early 1642.

During the first six months of the Long Parliament, hostility was directed primarily against Charles I's advisers. The leading officials of the Personal Rule, especially Strafford and Archbishop Laud, were bitterly denounced. This encouraged one of the puritan 'martyrs' of the 1630s, Robert Leighton, to petition against his conviction in Star Chamber for printing and distributing unlicensed pamphlets. A parliamentary committee, containing such leading figures as John Pym, John Hampden and Oliver St John, was immediately appointed to review his case. Shortly afterwards, another of the puritan 'martyrs', John Lilburne, followed Leighton's example. D'Ewes recorded that it was Cromwell who presented Lilburne's petition to the House of Commons [1.2].

**1.2**

November 9 . . . 1640: . . . Mr Cromwell delivered the petition of John Lilburne [complaining of] a sentence against him in Star Chamber etc. As whipping of 200 stripes [ = lashes] from Westminster to the Fleet. He was wounded by the Warden of the Fleet's men. His cause was referred to the committee of Dr Leighton's cause, and freedom was given him to follow his cause.

Documents 1.2–1.5 may all be found in the British Library, Harleian MS 162 (parliamentary diary of Sir Simonds D'Ewes). For printed versions, see *The Journal of Sir Simonds D'Ewes from the Beginning of the Long Parliament to the Opening of the Trial of the Earl of Strafford*, ed. W. Notestein (New Haven, 1923); and *The Private Journals of the Long Parliament, 3 January to 5 March 1642*, ed. W.H. Coates, A.S. Young and V.F. Snow (New Haven and London, 1982)

But this initiative was unsuccessful: Lilburne had to wait until 1646 before he received compensation for his Star Chamber fine. A much more successful intervention came on 30 December 1640 [1.3], when Cromwell moved the second reading of a bill for annual Parliaments.

**1.3**

December 30 . . . 1640: . . . Then Mr Cromwell moved that the bill touching the holding of a Parliament every year whether the King sends out his writ or not which Mr Strode preferred[1] might be read the second time, and so it was. Divers [MPs] spoke for the furthering of the said bill . . . and so it was ordered to be committed.

[1] 'which Mr Strode preferred': William Strode, MP for Berealston (Devon) and a future Parliamentarian, had introduced the bill for annual Parliaments six days earlier.

This bill ultimately became the Triennial Act (15 February 1641), which obliged the King to summon a Parliament at least every third year. However, Cromwell's fiery temper (already evident in 1630) made many of his early parliamentary speeches counter-productive. 1.4 is taken from D'Ewes's diary for 9 February 1641, and describes how Cromwell's intemperate remarks on episcopacy nearly led to his being called to the bar of the House. This was a sort of parliamentary 'excommunication', usually reserved for very serious offences.

**1.4**

February 9 . . . 1641: . . . Some would have the question of episcopacy put. Sir John Strangeways[1] rose up and spoke on their behalf, saying [that] if we made a parity in the church we must at last come to a parity in the commonwealth. And that the bishops were one of the three estates of the kingdom and had a voice in Parliament. Mr Cromwell stood up next and said [that] he knew no reason of those suppositions 5 and inferences which the gentleman had made that last spake; upon this divers interrupted and [demanded that he be] called . . . to the bar . . . Mr Cromwell went on, and said he did not understand why the gentleman that last spoke should make an inference of parity from the church to the commonwealth, nor that there was any necessity of the great revenues of bishops. He was more convinced touching the 10 irregularity of bishops than ever before, because like the Roman hierarchy, they would not endure to have their condition come to a trial.

[1] 'Sir John Strangeways': MP for Weymouth and Melcombe Regis (Dorset), and a future Royalist.

During the spring and summer of 1641 the future of episcopacy became a deeply divisive issue. These months also saw worrying signs (in the first Army

Plot and the Scottish 'Incident') that Charles was prepared to use military force against Parliament. News of the Irish Rebellion, which arrived on 1 November, posed the immediate problem of whether or not the King could be trusted to lead an army against the rebels. On 6 November Cromwell moved that the Earl of Essex might have 'power to assemble at all times the trained bands of the kingdom . . . for the defence thereof'. Then, on 4 January 1642, the King's abortive attempt to arrest five members of the House of Commons and Lord Mandeville confirmed all Cromwell's worst fears. Ten days later, Cromwell moved for a committee to discuss emergency defence measures [1.5]. This committee eventually drafted the Militia Ordinance (5 March 1642), which vested supreme military authority in the two Houses of Parliament rather than the King.

### 1.5

January 14 . . . 1642: . . . Mr Cromwell moved that a committee might be named to consider of means to put the kingdom in a posture of defence, which after two or three more had spoken to it was done, to meet in [the] Court of Wards[1] tomorrow at 7 of the clock.

[1] 'Court of Wards' = royal financial court administering wardships in Crown hands, and adjacent to the House of Commons.

Between March and August 1642 England drifted into civil war. Parliament mobilised forces under the Militia Ordinance; Charles retaliated by issuing commissions of array asserting his right to supreme military command. The first Civil War formally began on 22 August when the King raised his standard at Nottingham. The weeks immediately before this saw a number of provincial skirmishes as a small minority of activists took up arms for King or for Parliament. Cromwell was one such activist. In July the Commons sent him to organise the local defence forces in the Cambridge/Ely area. Acting without a specific military commission, Cromwell seized the castle at Cambridge and prevented the colleges from sending plate to the King's headquarters at York. **1.6** is an extract from *The Journal of the House of Commons*, and records Sir Philip Stapleton's announcement of Cromwell's actions to the House on 15 August.

### 1.6

Sir Philip Stapleton[1] gave an account, from the Committee for the Defence of the Kingdom, how the troops and forces of the Parliament are disposed of . . . Mr Cromwell, in Cambridgeshire, has seized the magazine in the castle at Cambridge;

and hath hindered the carrying of the plate from that university; which, as some report, was to the value of twenty thousand pounds, or thereabouts.

[1] 'Sir Philip Stapleton': MP for Boroughbridge (Yorkshire), and a Parliamentarian in the Civil War.

*The Journal of the House of Commons* vol. II, 15 August 1642 (London, 1803)


## Questions

1   Explain and comment on the following phrases:
    (i) 'like the Roman hierarchy' [1.4, line 11]
    (ii) 'to put the kingdom in a posture of defence' [1.5, line 2].
2   What does 1.1 reveal about Cromwell's *character*?
3   What can we learn from 1.2–1.5 about Cromwell's attitudes towards:
    (i)  the powers of Parliament
    (ii) religious issues
    (iii) the use of force against the King?
    Is there any evidence in the documents that these attitudes changed during the course of 1640–2? Explain your answer.
4   From the evidence in 1.2–1.5, how influential do you think Cromwell was as a member of the Long Parliament between 1640 and 1642? Explain your answer.
5   Discuss the *legality* of Cromwell's actions as described in 1.6.
6   Using the evidence in 1.1–1.6, and your wider reading, speculate on why Cromwell was willing to take up arms for Parliament in the summer of 1642.


During 1642 and 1643 Cromwell rapidly established himself as an exceptionally zealous and gifted military leader. In 1643 he was promoted to colonel, and took part in at least eight sieges and battles. On 2 July 1644 he played a vital role in Parliament's victory at the battle of Marston Moor. Yet despite his conspicuous success in the field, his enemies were not confined to the Royalist party. The Parliamentarians who disapproved of Cromwell's conduct included Edward Montague, second Earl of Manchester, commander of the Eastern Association army, with whom he had already clashed over fen drainage. Documents 1.7–1.10 tell the story of a major row between them which erupted late in 1644. On 25 November, in the House of Commons, Cromwell accused Manchester of deliberately missing opportunities to inflict losses on the

Royalists [1.7]. Manchester replied in the House of Lords on 28 November with a series of allegations against Cromwell. He put these in writing a few days later [1.8]. Meanwhile, a Commons committee had been appointed to investigate the quarrel. 1.9, a 'statement by an opponent of Cromwell' in the Eastern Association army, is taken from the body of evidence which Manchester assembled, while 1.10 is part of the testimony given by the Parliamentarian MP and officer Sir Arthur Haselrig before the Commons committee on 6 December.

## 1.7

Being commanded by the House [of Commons] to give an account concerning the many opportunities lost and advantages given to the enemy since the late conjunction of our armies which seemed to be by some miscarriage or neglect in the conduct of the armies . . . I did . . . freely declare that I thought the Earl of Manchester was most in fault for most of those miscarriages and the ill                  5
consequences of them. And because I had a great deal of reason to think that his Lordship's miscarriage in these particulars was neither through accidents (which could not be helped) nor through his improvidence only, but through his backwardness to all action, and . . . that backwardness was not merely from dullness or indisposedness [ = disinclination] to engagement, but . . . from . . . unwillingness   10
to have this war prosecuted unto a full victory, and a design or desire to have it ended by accommodation, and that on such terms to which it might be disadvantageous to bring the King too low. To the end therefore that . . . the state might not be further deceived [ = disappointed] in their expectations from their army, I did (in the faithful discharge of my duty to the Parliament and kingdom)    15
freely discover [ = reveal] those . . . apprehensions.

'Cromwell's Narrative' [25 November 1644], in *The Quarrel between the Earl of Manchester and Oliver Cromwell*, ed. J. Bruce and D. Masson (Camden Society, second series, vol. XII, 1875)

## 1.8

Of late I have not given so free and full a power unto [Cromwell] as formerly I did, because I heard that he used his power so as in honour I could not avow him in it . . . for his expressions were sometimes against the nobility, that he hoped to live to see never a nobleman in England, and he loved such [and such] better than others because they did not love lords. And he further expressed himself with contempt of    5
the Assembly of Divines,[1] to whom I pay a reverence, as to the most learned and godly convention that has been these many ages, yet these he termed persecutors, and that they persecuted honester men than themselves. His animosity against the Scottish nation, whom I affect [ = like] as joined with us in [the] *Solemn League and Covenant*,[2] and honour as jointly instrumental with us in the common cause; yet   10

against these his animosity was such as he told me that in the way they now carried themselves, pressing for their [church] discipline, he could as soon draw his sword against them as against any in the King's army; and he grew so pressing for his designs as he told me that he . . . desired to have none in my army but such as were of the Independent judgement,[3] giving me this reason: that in case there should be     15
propositions for peace or any conclusion of a peace such as might not stand with those ends that honest men should aim at, this army might prevent such a mischief.

[1] 'the Assembly of Divines' = the Westminster Assembly, established by Parliament on 12 June 1643 to draw up plans for a Presbyterian Church in England.
[2] '*Solemn League and Covenant*' = the treaty between the English Parliament and the Scots, 25 September 1643.
[3] '[those] of the Independent judgement' = those opposed to a national church, who believed that each congregation should be independent.

**'A Letter from the Earl of Manchester to the House of Lords',**
**[?2] December 1644, ed. S.R. Gardiner, in** *Camden Miscellany*, **vol. VIII**
**(Camden Society, second series, vol. XXXI, 1883)**

### 1.9

Colonel Cromwell [chooses for] his officers not such as were soldiers or men of estate, but such as were common men, poor and of mean parentage, only he would give them the title of godly, precious men; yet his common practice was to cashier honest gentlemen and soldiers that were stout in the cause . . . I have heard him often . . . say that it must not be soldiers nor [the] Scots that must do this work, but     5
it must be the godly to this purpose. When any new Englishman or some new upstart Independent[1] did appear there must be a way made for them by cashiering others, some honest commander or other, and those silly people put in their command . . . If you look upon his own regiment of horses see what a swarm there is of those that call themselves the godly. Some of them profess they have seen visions     10
and had revelations . . . But for the absolute Independent he is cruel without mercy, covetous without measure.

[1] 'Independent': see 1.8, note 3.

**'Statement by an opponent of Cromwell', in** *The Quarrel between the Earl of Manchester and Oliver Cromwell*, **ed. J. Bruce and D. Masson (Camden Society, second series, vol. XII, 1875)**

### 1.10

The Earl of Manchester said . . . 'That if we beat the King ninety and nine times yet he is King still, and so will his posterity be after him, but if the King beat us once we shall be all hanged, and our posterity made slaves'. These were the very words as this examinant remembers, but he is sure words to this effect the Earl of Manchester there[1] used as a motive against present engaging. Whereupon     5

Lieutenant-General Cromwell replied, 'My Lord, if this be so, why did we take up arms at first? This is against fighting ever hereafter; if so, let us make peace, be it never so base'.

¹ 'there' = at the siege of Shaw House, Yorkshire, in October 1644.

**Deposition of Sir Arthur Haselrig, 6 December 1644: Public Record Office, SP 16/503/56.IX**

## Questions

1   What is being referred to in the phrase 'the late conjunction of our armies' [1.7, lines 2–3]?
2   Are 1.8 and 1.9 presenting a common picture of Cromwell? If so, what is it? If not, in what ways do they differ? Explain your answer.
3   To what extent and in what ways does the evidence given in 1.10 bear out:
     (i) Cromwell's allegations in 1.7
     (ii) Manchester's allegations in 1.8
     (iii) the claims made in 1.9?
4   Using the material in 1.7–1.10, summarise Cromwell's attitude towards:
     (i) Parliament's prosecution of the first Civil War
     (ii) the Scots
     (iii) promotions within the Parliamentarian forces.
5   Does the picture of Cromwell which emerges in 1.7–1.10 confirm or conflict with that which you have encountered earlier in this chapter, and in your wider reading? Justify your response.
6   Does anything in 1.7–1.10 suggest that a 'new modelling' of the Parliamentarian army was necessary by the autumn of 1644?

Cromwell was clearly someone who inspired strong feelings in friends and enemies alike. The next three documents [1.11–1.13] illustrate how these feelings were expressed in Royalist and Parliamentarian propaganda during the first Civil War. We begin with an extract from the Royalist weekly newspaper *Mercurius Aulicus* [1.11], describing Cromwell's visit to Peterborough in April 1643:

**1.11**

It was advertised [ = reported] this day [ = 28 April 1643] from Peterborough that Colonel Cromwell had bestowed a visit on that little city and put them to the charge of his entertainment, plundering a great part thereof to discharge the reckoning,¹

and further that in pursuance of the thorough Reformation, he did most miserably
deface the Cathedral church, break down the organs, and destroy the glass windows,   5
committing many other outrages on the house of God, which were not acted by the
Goths in the sack of Rome,[2] and are most commonly forborn by the Turks[3] when
they possess themselves by force of a Christian city.

[1] 'to discharge the reckoning' = to settle the account.
[2] 'the Goths in the sack of Rome' = Germanic tribe which sacked Rome in 410 and became
synonymous with barbarity.
[3] 'the Turks' = Muslims, associated at that time with tyranny and paganism.

*Mercurius Aulicus*, 17th week (23–9 April 1643)

However, many Parliamentarian writers saw Cromwell in a rather different
light. **1.12** is taken from a four-part military history of the first Civil War by the
Parliamentarian propagandist John Vicars, and recounts Cromwell's role in the
battle of Marston Moor:

**1.12**

As for that famous and magnanimous commander, Lieutenant-General Cromwell,
whose prowess and prudence, as they have rendered him most renowned for many
former successful deeds of chivalry, so in this fight they have crowned him with the
never withering laurels of fame and honour, who with so lion-like courage and
impregnable animosity, charged his proudest adversaries again and again, like a    5
Roman Marcellus[1] indeed, undauntedly out-daring and overbearing his stoutest
popish and atheistical antagonists, even to the end of the fight; and at last came off,
as with some wounds, so with honour and triumph inferior to none.

[1] 'Marcellus' = Roman general, described by Livy as 'the sword of Rome'.

**John Vicars, *Magnalia Dei Anglicana. Or England's Parliamentary-Chronicle*,
part III (London, 1646)**

Such military skills made Cromwell indispensable to the Parliamentarians. In
the years between 1642 and 1651 he was never defeated in battle. Yet on 3 April
1645 his military future was jeopardised by Parliament's Self-Denying
Ordinance. This stated that all members of both Houses of Parliament should
cease to hold civil and military offices, and thus paved the way for the creation
of the New Model Army. But Cromwell's military prestige was such that
Parliament was prepared to exempt him from the provisions of this ordinance.
Joshua Sprigge, one of the chaplains of the New Model Army, takes up the
story:

1.13

Lieutenant-General Cromwell . . . a member of the House of Commons, long
famous for godliness and zeal to his country, of great note for his service in the
House, accepted of a commission at the very beginning of this war, wherein he
served his country faithfully, and it was observed God was with him, and he began
to be renowned. Insomuch that men found that the narrow room, whereunto his    5
first employments had confined their thoughts, must be enlarged to an expectation
of greater things and higher employments, whereunto divine providence had
designed him for the good of this kingdom. When the time therefore drew near that
he, as the rest had done, should lay down his commission upon a new ordinance,[1]
the House considering how God had blessed their affairs under his hand, thought fit  10
to dispense with his absence from the House.

[1] 'new ordinance' = the Self-Denying Ordinance, 3 April 1645.

**Joshua Sprigge,** *Anglia Rediviva* **(London, 1647)**

## Questions

1  Explain and comment on the following phrases:
   (i) 'in pursuance of the thorough Reformation' [**1.11, line 4**]
   (ii) 'popish and atheistical antagonists' [**1.12, line 7**].
2  What may be gleaned from **1.11–1.13** about:
   (i) Cromwell's religious attitudes
   (ii) Cromwell's attitudes towards Parliament
   (iii) Cromwell's attitudes towards the first Civil War
   (iv) Royalists during the first Civil War
   (v) Parliamentarians during the first Civil War?
3  What do **1.11–1.13** agree about in their accounts of Cromwell? What do
   they disagree about?
4  Discuss the value as historical evidence of each of **1.11–1.13**. What
   problems might such sources pose for the historian?

During 1645–6, Cromwell received a series of exemptions from the Self-
Denying Ordinance lasting for between forty days and six months at a time.
These years saw the decisive Parliamentarian victory at the battle of Naseby
(14 June 1645) and the final surrender of the Royalists at Oxford (24 June
1646). Parliament then offered Charles peace terms (the Newcastle Propositions) which included the demand that a Presbyterian Church be established in

England. These negotiations reached deadlock and in the summer of 1647 the Army Council presented alternative terms, known as the *Heads of the Proposals* [1.14]. Cromwell strongly supported these, and they therefore throw some light on the sort of settlement which he wanted to see.

**1.14**

I. That . . . a certain period may (by Act of Parliament) be set for the ending of this Parliament . . . That Parliaments may biennially be called and meet at a certain day, with such provision for the certainty thereof, as in the late Act was made for triennial Parliaments . . . II. That the power of the militia by sea and land, during the space of ten years next ensuing, shall be ordered and disposed by the Lords and 5 Commons assembled, and to be assembled in the Parliament or Parliaments of England, by such persons as they shall nominate and appoint for that purpose . . . IV. That an Act be passed for disposing the great offices for ten years by the Lords and Commons in Parliament . . . XI. An Act to be passed to take away all coercive power, authority, and jurisdiction of bishops and all other ecclesiastical officers 10 whatsoever, extending to any civil penalties upon any . . . XII. That there be a repeal of all the Acts . . . enjoining the use of the Book of Common Prayer, and imposing any penalties for neglect thereof; as also of all Acts . . . imposing any penalty for not coming to church, or for meetings elsewhere for prayer or other religious duties . . . XIII. That the taking of the Covenant be not enforced upon 15 any, nor any penalties imposed upon the refusers, whereby men might be restrained to take it against their judgements or consciences . . . XIV. That . . . his Majesty's person, his Queen, and royal issue may be restored to a condition of safety, honour and freedom in this nation, without diminution to their personal rights, or further limitation to the exercise of the regal power than according to the particulars 20 foregoing . . . XVI. That . . . a general Act of Oblivion [may] extend unto all . . . to absolve from all trespasses, misdemeanours etc. done in prosecution of the war . . .

'The Heads of the Proposals agreed upon by his Excellency Sir Thomas Fairfax and the Council of the Army', 1 August 1647, in *The Constitutional Documents of the Puritan Revolution, 1625–1660*, ed. S.R. Gardiner (Oxford, 1899)

However, Charles was determined to play Parliament and the army off against each other. He did not accept the *Heads of the Proposals*, and on 9 September he bluntly refused the Newcastle Propositions. On 21–3 September the Commons discussed what to do next. A manuscript newsletter [1.15], written to Hyde on 27 September, reported Cromwell's opinion. Another letter [1.16] indicated the response of Henry Marten, a committed republican.

**1.15**

His Majesty's answer to the propositions . . . [was] voted to be a denial . . .
Whereupon a sharp debate grew [over] whether the King should be sent unto any
more, or whether they should forthwith proceed to the settlement of the kingdom.
To the latter most of the orators inclined, and in likelihood would have led the
House [of Commons] that way, but . . . it was opposed by Cromwell and Ireton,[1]     5
who said it was no fit time to proceed with such vigour . . . There have been in the
prosecution of this business some desperate motions; [such] as that the King, in
regard that many who give him ill counsel and are professed enemies to the
Parliament resort unto him, should be restrained; that they should think no more of
the King, but proceed as if there were no such thing in the world; for . . . he is     10
always an impediment to all good resolutions . . . But all those speeches have been
stopped by Cromwell and Ireton,[1] whose civilities are visible, but the reality of their
intention not clearly discerned.

[1] 'Ireton' = Henry Ireton, Parliamentarian MP and Commissary-General, probable author
of the *Heads of the Proposals*, and Cromwell's son-in-law.

**Letter of intelligence, 27 September 1647, in the Bodleian Library,
MS Clarendon 30/1**

**1.16**

Cromwell, Ireton[1] and Huntington[2] are still the same; insomuch that Henry
Marten, that *flagellum principium*,[3] said publicly that Cromwell was king-ridden.

[1] 'Ireton': see **1.15, note 1**.
[2] 'Huntington' = Major Robert Huntington, the second-in-command of Cromwell's
regiment, who was committed to a settlement with the King, and turned against Cromwell in
1648 (see **4.17**).
[3] '*flagellum principium*' = scourge of princes.

**Nathaniel Hobart to John Hobart, [? September or October] 1647, in the
Bodleian Library, MS Tanner 58**

But on 11 November 1647 the King escaped from army custody at Hampton
Court and fled to the Isle of Wight. This strengthened his growing reputation
for duplicity. On 29 November the Royalist moderate Sir John Berkeley
investigated the possibility of further negotiations between Charles and the
army. In his *Memoirs* [**1.17**], Berkeley described Cromwell's response:

**1.17**

The next morning [= 29 November 1647] I sent Colonel Cook[1] to Cromwell, to let him know that I had letters and instructions to him from the King. He sent me word by the same messenger, that he dared not see me, it being very dangerous to us both, and bid me be assured that he would serve his Majesty as long as he could do it without his own ruin; but desired that I would not expect that he should            5
perish for his [= the King's] sake.

[1] 'Colonel Cook' = probably the Royalist Colonel Francis Cook.

*Memoirs of Sir John Berk[e]ley* (London, 1699)

Meanwhile Charles, unwilling to accept the terms offered by either Parliament or the army, opened negotiations with the Scots. The latter deeply resented Parliament's failure to honour its agreement (in the *Solemn League and Covenant* of 1643) to establish an English Church modelled on the Scottish Presbyterian Kirk. The result was the Engagement (26 December 1647), whereby the Scots promised if necessary to send an army to force Parliament to accept the King's terms. The next day, Charles rejected outright Parliament's latest peace offer, the *Four Bills*. A week later, on 3 January 1648, the House of Commons decided to pass a 'Vote of No Addresses' forbidding any further negotiations with the King. 1.18 is taken from the diary of John Boys, MP for Kent, and records Cromwell's speech during the debate which preceded the vote.

**1.18**

We declared our intentions [to preserve] monarchy, and they still are so, unless necessity enforce an alteration. It's granted the King has broken his trust, yet you are fearful to declare you will make no further addresses. Where will the people know to have you? A not owning of God in these troubles hath caused a protraction of the war . . . Look on the people you represent, and break not your trust, and            5
expose not the honest party of the kingdom, who have bled for you, and suffer not misery to fall upon them for want of courage and resolution in you, else the honest people may take such courses as nature dictates to them.

**British Library, Additional MS 50200 (parliamentary diary of John Boys, entry for 3 January 1648). For a printed version, see 'The Diary of John Boys, 1647–8', ed. D. Underdown, *Bulletin of the Institute of Historical Research* XXXIX (1966)**

## Questions

1   Explain and comment on the following phrases:
    (i) 'the late Act . . . for triennial Parliaments' [**1.14, lines 3–4**]
    (ii) 'the honest party of the kingdom' [**1.18, line 6**]
    (iii) 'such courses as nature dictates to them' [**1.18, line 8**].
2   What can we learn from **1.14** about Cromwell's attitudes in the summer of
    1647 towards:
    (i) Parliament
    (ii) the Church and religious issues
    (iii) the King
    (iv) the first Civil War?
3   What is Cromwell's attitude towards the King in **1.15**? Is it consistent with
    that indicated in **1.14**? If not, in what ways do they differ? Explain your
    answer.
4   Do **1.14** and **1.15** provide evidence for the charge made in **1.16**? Explain
    your answer.
5   What is Cromwell's attitude towards the King in **1.17**? Has it changed in
    any way from those revealed earlier? If so, how?
6   In a letter written to his cousin Robert Hammond on the evening of 3
    January 1648, Cromwell described the 'Vote of No Addresses' as 'a mighty
    providence to the kingdom and to us all'. Does **1.18** help to explain what he
    meant by this?
7   What may be gleaned from **1.18** about Cromwell's attitudes in January
    1648 towards:
    (i) Parliament's role
    (ii) the King?
8   'The King's flight [to the Isle of Wight], and the revelations of his intrigues
    with the Scots which followed, showed Cromwell on what a rotten
    foundation he had based his policy [of negotiating with the King]' (C.H.
    Firth, *Dictionary of National Biography*, vol. XIII). Discuss and debate
    with reference to **1.14–1.18**.


In order to win the first Civil War, Parliament had to raise vast quantities of
men, money and arms. This was done through a series of oppressive county
committees which imposed heavy taxes (the excise, the assessments) and
frequently resorted to arbitrary arrest and imprisonment of those who resisted.
Furthermore, the outlawing of the Prayer Book and the abolition of traditional
Anglican festivals such as Christmas and Easter were widely resented. The

spring and summer of 1648 saw a sequence of provincial revolts (especially in Kent, East Anglia, Yorkshire and South Wales) against this new 'Roundhead tyranny'. Charles increased the pressure on Parliament by engineering a Scottish invasion under the terms of the Engagement. The following documents [**1.19–1.24**] illustrate Cromwell's response to these events, which became known as the second Civil War.

In April 1648, the officers of the New Model Army held a prayer meeting at Windsor Castle. One of them, William Allen, later recounted Cromwell's contribution:

### 1.19

Lieutenant-General Cromwell did press very earnestly on all there present, to a thorough consideration of our actions as an army, as well as our ways particularly [= individually], as private Christians, to see if any iniquity could be found in them; and what it was, that if possible we might find it out, and so remove the cause of such sad rebukes as were upon us by reason of our iniquities . . . [We] review[ed]    5
our actions again, by which means we were, by a gracious hand of the Lord, led to find out the very steps . . . by which we had departed from the Lord, and provoked him to depart from us; which we found to be those cursed carnal conferences, [which] our own wisdom, fears and want of faith had prompted us the year before to entertain with the King and his party . . . [God] did direct our steps, and presently    10
we were led and helped to a clear agreement among ourselves, not any dissenting, that it was the duty of our day, with the forces we had, to go out and fight against those potent enemies which that year in all places appeared against us, with a humble confidence in the name of the Lord only, that we should destroy them; also enabling us then, after serious seeking his face, to come to a very clear and joint    15
resolution . . . that it was our duty, if ever the Lord brought us back again in peace, to call Charles Stuart, that man of blood, to an account for that blood he had shed, and mischief he had done to his utmost, against the Lord's cause and people in these poor nations.

**William Allen,** *A Faithful Memorial of that Remarkable Meeting of Many Officers of the Army* **(London, 1659), reprinted in John, Baron Somers,** *A Collection of Scarce and Valuable Tracts,* **ed. Sir Walter Scott, vol. VI (London, 1811)**

The 'revolt of the provinces' in 1648 was very poorly co-ordinated, and Parliament was able to defeat each local uprising in turn. The Scots, who invaded England in July, initially posed a more serious threat, but Cromwell routed them at the battle of Preston (17–19 August). **1.20** is taken from Cromwell's letter to the Speaker of the House of Commons, dated 20 August. Another letter [**1.21**], written to two MPs on 20 November, summarises Cromwell's view of the second Civil War.

**I.20**

Surely, Sir, this[1] is nothing but the hand of God, and wherever anything in this world is exalted, or exalts itself, God will pull it down, for this is the day wherein He alone will be exalted. It is not fit for me to give advice, nor to say a word which use should be made of this, more than to pray you, and all that acknowledge God, that they would exalt Him, and not hate His people, who are as the apple of His eye, 5 and for whom even Kings shall be reproved; and that you would take courage to do the work of the Lord, in fulfilling the end of your magistracy, in seeking the peace and welfare of the people of this land.

[1] 'this' = Cromwell's victory at the battle of Preston.

**Cromwell to William Lenthall, Speaker of the House of Commons, 20 August 1648, in Carlyle vol. I**

**I.21**

The House of Commons did vote all those traitors that did adhere to, or bring in, the Scots in their late invading of this kingdom under [the] Duke [of] Hamilton,[1] and not without very clear justice, this being a more prodigious treason than any that had been perpetrated before. Because the former quarrel on their part was that Englishmen might rule over one another; this to vassalise us to a foreign nation. 5 And their fault who have appeared in this summer's business [ = the second Civil War] is certainly double to theirs who were in the first, because it is the repetition of the same offence against all the witnesses that God has borne, by making and abetting to a second war.

[1] 'Hamilton' = James, Duke of Hamilton, Scottish Royalist and commander of the Scottish army which invaded England in July 1648.

**Cromwell to Robert Jenner and John Ashe, 20 November 1648, in Carlyle vol. I**

Yet it soon became clear that the second Civil War had solved nothing. Most people were still unable to envisage a settlement which did not involve the King. Parliament therefore repealed the 'Vote of No Addresses' on 2 September, and a fortnight later reopened negotiations with Charles I at Newport on the Isle of Wight. The terms offered to the King were essentially unchanged since 1642. However, a tiny minority, consisting mostly of army leaders, regarded these negotiations as a betrayal of the 'cause' for which they had fought. They became convinced that a lasting settlement could only be achieved by removing the King. Cromwell expressed his own feelings about the Newport talks in a letter [**I.22**] to his cousin, Robert Hammond, on 25 November 1648.

1.22

Dost thou not think this fear of the Levellers (of whom there is no fear) that they would destroy nobility, had caused some to rake up corruption; to find it lawful to make this ruining hypocritical agreement [ = the Treaty of Newport], on one part? Hath not this biased even some good men? . . . Have not some of our friends . . . been occasioned to overlook what is just and honest, and to think the people of God  5 may have as much or more good the one way than the other? Good by this man [ = Charles I], against whom the Lord hath witnessed, and whom thou knowest. Is this so in their hearts; or is it reasoned, forced in?

**Cromwell to Colonel Robert Hammond, 25 November 1648, in Carlyle vol. I**

Nevertheless, on 5 December the House of Commons voted by 129 to 83 to continue negotiations with the King. This was too much for the radicals in the army. The next morning, Colonel Pride's musketeers excluded about 110 MPs from the House, while another 160 withdrew in protest. Cromwell was besieging Pontefract (Yorkshire) and only reached London on the evening of 6 December. In January 1649 the 'Rump' of the Commons (now containing fewer than eighty MPs) appointed a High Court of Justice to try the King. This passed sentence on 27 January, and Cromwell was one of fifty-nine members of the High Court who signed Charles's death warrant, dated 29 January. When Charles II was restored in 1660, some of the other 'regicides', such as Richard Ingoldsby, claimed that Cromwell had physically forced them to sign the warrant [1.23]. However, during the 1660s the widow of another 'regicide', Colonel John Hutchinson, wrote a quite different account of these events [1.24].

1.23

[Colonel Richard Ingoldsby stated that] it is very true he was named amongst those who were appointed to be judges of the King; and it is as true that he was never once present with them, always abhorring the action in his heart, and having no other passion in any part of the quarrel but his personal kindness to Cromwell. The next day after the horrid sentence was pronounced [ = 28 January 1649], he had  5 occasion to speak with an officer who, he was told, was in the Painted Chamber;[1] where, when he came thither, he saw Cromwell, and the rest of those who had sat upon the King, and were then, as he found afterwards, assembled to sign the warrant for his Majesty's death. As soon as Cromwell's eyes were upon him, he ran to him, and taking him by the hand, drew him by force to the table; and said,  10 though he had escaped him all the while, he should now sign that paper as well as they. Which [Ingoldsby], seeing what it was, refused with great passion, saying he knew nothing of the business . . . But Cromwell and others held him by violence; and Cromwell, with a loud laughter, taking his hand in his, and putting the pen between his fingers, with his own hand wrote *Richard Ingol[d]sby*, he making all the  15 resistance he could. And he said, if his name there were compared with what he had ever written himself, it could never be looked upon as his own hand.

¹ 'the Painted Chamber' = a large room in the Palace of Westminster, situated between the House of Lords and the House of Commons.

**Edward Hyde, Earl of Clarendon, *The History of the Rebellion and Civil Wars in England*, ed. W.D. Macray, book XVI, section 225 (Oxford, 1888)**

1.24

Some of [the regicides] afterwards, for excuse, belied [ = lied about] themselves, and said they were under the awe of the army, and overpersuaded by Cromwell and the like. But it is certain that all men herein were left to their free liberty of acting, neither persuaded nor compelled; and as there were some nominated [to the High Court of Justice] that never sat, and others who sat at first, but dared not hold on,  5 so all the rest might have declined it if they would, when it is apparent they would have suffered nothing by so doing . . . [In 1660], when it came to Ingoldsby's turn, he, with many tears, professed his repentance for that murder, and told a false tale how Cromwell held his hand, and forced him to subscribe the sentence, and made a most whining recantation . . . Colonel Hutchinson . . . [said] . . . 'That for his  10 actings in those days, if he had erred, it was the inexperience of his age, and the defect of his judgement . . .'

*Memoirs of the Life of Colonel Hutchinson . . . Written by his Widow Lucy*, ed. J. Hutchinson (London, 1806)

## Questions

1   Explain and comment on the following phrases:
    (i) 'those cursed carnal conferences' [**1.19, line 8**]
    (ii) 'fulfilling the end of your magistracy' [**1.20, line 7**]
    (iii) 'this ruining hypocritical agreement' [**1.22, line 3**]
    (iv) 'this man, against whom the Lord hath witnessed'
         [**1.22, lines 6–7**].
2   What can be learnt from **1.19–1.22** about Cromwell's attitudes towards:
    (i) the second Civil War
    (ii) the Scots
    (iii) the battle of Preston
    (iv) Parliament
    (v) the King?

3   How far do **1.19–1.22** help you to explain the events leading to the trial of Charles I? Justify your response.

4   How do you account for the contradiction between **1.23** and **1.24**? On which of these documents would you place more weight, and why?

5   There is a legend that Cromwell later described the regicide as a 'cruel necessity'. How plausible do you find this story in the light of the evidence in this chapter?

6   Is it possible to discern any consistent aims in Cromwell's career as a soldier and politician during the 1640s? Explain your answer.

# 2 Cromwell's political attitudes

On 30 January 1649, Charles I was beheaded; on 17 March the monarchy was abolished as 'unnecessary, burdensome and dangerous to the liberty, safety and public interest of the people'. Finally, on 19 May England was declared to be 'a Commonwealth or Free-State'. From this time until his death on 3 September 1658 Cromwell was the dominant figure in England's only republican experiment. He wielded more power than any other English commoner before or since. On 16 December 1653, he was created Lord Protector of England, Scotland and Ireland, an office which he held for the rest of his life. Many of his contemporaries regarded him as king in all but name. Indeed, during the 1650s rumours abounded that Cromwell would shortly assume the title of king; yet when a formal offer was finally made in 1657 he declined after months of agonised indecision. After his death, he was given an elaborate State funeral modelled on that of James I.

This chapter seeks to unravel the political attitudes and objectives which lay behind Cromwell's extraordinary career. It is divided into six sections. We will look first at his basic assumptions about the nature of politics and about his own role within it. Then we will explore Cromwell's concept of the 'fundamentals' of government: what did he mean by this phrase, and how far did his rule rest on coercion or consent? The two central sections consider Cromwell's attitudes towards Parliament and the kingship. Did he pursue a vision of liberty or was he a ruthless tyrant? How persuasive are Cromwell's justifications of his own actions? The fifth section examines various contemporary perceptions of Cromwell. Here we will look at several accounts which argue that Cromwell possessed no coherent political principles, but was motivated throughout by ambition and self-interest. The chapter concludes with some visual images of Cromwell and his government taken from coins, seals and woodcuts.

The first two documents [2.1 and 2.2] both throw light on Cromwell's view of politics in general, and of his own political role in particular. 2.1 is extracted from Cromwell's addresses at the Army Council debates at Putney in October–November 1647, and reveals much about his attitude to political institutions. 2.2, drawn from a speech to representatives of the second Protectorate Parliament in April 1657, explains how Cromwell saw his own place within English politics.

**2.1**

They [ = the people] may have some jealousies and apprehensions that we
[ = himself] are wedded and glued to forms of government . . . You will find that we
are far from being so particularly engaged . . . If you make the best of it, if you
should change the government to the best of it, it is but a moral thing. It is but as
Paul says 'dross and dung in comparison of Christ'.

**Cromwell at the Putney Debates, 28 October–1 November 1647, in Carlyle
vol. III**

**2.2**

I am a man standing in the place I am in; which place I undertook not so much out
of the hope of doing any good, as out of a desire to prevent mischief and evil, which
I did see was imminent in the nation . . . We were running headlong into confusion
and disorder, and would necessarily have run into blood . . . I profess I had not that
apprehension when I undertook the place, that I could do much good, but I did          5
think I might prevent imminent evil . . . I am ready to serve not as a King, but as a
constable if you like! For truly I have, as before God, thought it often that I could
not tell what my business was, nor what I was in the place I stood in, save
comparing myself to a good constable set to keep the peace of the parish. And truly
this hath been my content and satisfaction in the troubles that I have undergone,          10
that yet you have peace.

**Cromwell to the representatives of the second Protectorate Parliament,
13 April 1657, in Carlyle vol. III**

## Questions

1   Explain and comment on the phrase 'wedded and glued to forms of
    government' [**2.1, line 2**].
2   Why might Cromwell have chosen to liken himself to 'a good constable'
    [**2.2, line 9**]?
3   Do the dates and audiences of **2.1** and **2.2** help in any way to explain their
    contents?

How did Cromwell apply these very broad ideas to England in the 1650s? The
next sequence of documents [2.3–2.6] opens up Cromwell's views on the nature
and purpose of the Interregnum governments. In his speech to the first
Protectorate Parliament on 12 September 1654 [2.3], he outlined what he called
the 'fundamentals' of government. Two-and-a-half years later, in a speech to

the representatives of the second Protectorate Parliament [2.4], he adopted a different approach which stressed the need to further 'the two greatest concernments which God hath in this world'. The second of these 'interests' was 'the civil liberty' of the people, a theme developed in 2.5, taken from Cromwell's closing speech to the first Protectorate Parliament on 22 January 1655. Here he argued that government should rest on 'the acceptation and consent of the people'. However, many of Cromwell's contemporaries believed that his rule rested less upon consent than upon coercion. These included the Venetian Secretary in England, Lorenzo Paulucci, who reported in February 1654 how Cromwell had cowed the English people into submission [2.6].

### 2.3

There are some things in this Establishment[1] that are fundamental . . . about which I shall deal plainly with you: they may not be parted with; but will, I trust, be delivered over to posterity, as being the fruits of our blood and travail. The Government by a Single Person and a Parliament is a fundamental. It is the *esse* [ = essence], it is constitutive. And as for the person, though I may seem to plead    5 for myself, yet I do not: no, nor can any reasonable man say it . . . I plead for this nation, and for all honest men therein . . . In every government there must be somewhat fundamental, somewhat like a *Magna Charta*, that should be standing and unalterable . . . That Parliaments should not make themselves perpetual is a fundamental. Of what assurance is a law to prevent so great an evil, if it lie in one or   10 the same legislature to unlaw it again. Is such a law as this like to be lasting? It will be like a rope of sand; it will give no security; for the same men may unbuild what they have built. Again, is not liberty of conscience in religion a fundamental? So long as there is liberty of conscience for the Supreme Magistrate to exercise his conscience in erecting what sort of church-government he is satisfied he should set   15 up, why should he not give . . . the like liberty to others? Liberty of conscience is a natural right . . . Liberty of conscience, truly that's a thing ought to be very reciprocal! . . . This, I say, is a fundamental.

[1] 'this Establishment' = *The Instrument of Government*, 16 December 1653.

**Cromwell to the first Protectorate Parliament, 12 September 1654, in Carlyle vol. II**

### 2.4

[The second Protectorate Parliament has] been zealous of the two greatest concernments which God hath in the world. The one is that of religion, and of the just preservation of the professors of it; to give them all due and just liberty; and to assert the truth of God . . . The other thing cared for is the civil liberty and interest

of the nation. Which though it is, and indeed I think ought to be, subordinate to a 5
more peculiar interest of God, yet it is the next best God hath given men in this
world; and if well cared-for, it is better than any rock to fence men in their own
interests . . . These are things I must acknowledge Christian and honourable . . .
And upon these two interests, if God shall account me worthy, I shall live and die.
And I must say, that if I were to give an account before a greater tribunal than any 10
earthly one, and if I were asked why I have engaged all along in the late war, I could
give no answer but it would be a wicked one if it did not comprehend these two
ends.

**Cromwell to the representatives of the second Protectorate Parliament,
3 April 1657, in Carlyle vol. III**


**2.5**

I desire not to keep my place in this government an hour longer than I may preserve
England in its just rights, and may protect the people of God in such a just liberty
of their consciences as I have already mentioned . . . This Government called you
hither, the constitution whereof being . . . a Single Person and a Parliament. And
this was thought most agreeable to the sense of the nation . . . I would not have 5
been averse to any alteration, of the good of which I might have been convinced,
although I could not have agreed to the taking it off the foundation on which it
stands, namely, the acceptation and consent of the people.

**Cromwell to the first Protectorate Parliament, 22 January 1655, in Carlyle
vol. II**


**2.6**

[Cromwell made a State visit to the City of London amid] all the outward signs of
respect and honour, but with very scanty marks of goodwill from the people in
general, who, on the contrary, greeted him with a rancour which increases daily
because he has arrogated to himself despotic authority and the actual sovereignty of
these realms under the mask of humility and the public service . . . Obedience and 5
submission were never so manifest in England as at present, the fear of coercion
under which they labour increasing with the remembrance of the tragical events of
the Civil Wars. Their spirits are so crushed and although they consider themselves
oppressed, dissatisfied and deluded, they dare not rebel and only murmur under
their breath, though all live in hope of the fulfilment one day of the prophecies 10
foretelling a change of rule ere long.

**Lorenzo Paulucci, Venetian Secretary in England, to Giovanni Sagredo,
Venetian Ambassador in France, 21 February 1654, in *Calendar of State
Papers Venetian*, ed. A.B. Hinds, vol. XXIX (1653–4)**

## Questions

1   What do you think Cromwell is referring to in the phrase 'that Parliaments should not make themselves perpetual is a fundamental' [**2.3, lines 9–10**]?
2   Use **2.3** to explain what Cromwell thought were 'the fundamentals' of government.
3   Use **2.4** to summarise what Cromwell thought were God's 'two greatest concernments'.
4   Is Cromwell advancing compatible arguments in **2.3** and **2.4**? If not, in what ways are they incompatible? Explain your answer and consider its implications.
5   Does **2.6** provide evidence against Cromwell's claim in **2.5**? Justify your answer.


In England before the Civil Wars, the people's consent had been expressed through their representatives in Parliament. What was Cromwell's attitude towards this institution? During the 1640s Cromwell fought in, and ultimately led, the army which the Long Parliament had created (see Chapter 1). He expressed his feelings towards that Parliament in September 1644 in a letter to his brother-in-law, Colonel Valentine Walton:

**2.7**

We study the glory of God, and the honour and liberty of the Parliament, for which we unanimously fight, without seeking our own interests . . . I profess I could never satisfy myself of the justness of this war, but from the authority of the Parliament to maintain itself in its rights; and in this cause I hope to approve myself an honest man and single-hearted.

**Cromwell to Colonel Valentine Walton, [? 5 or 6] September 1644, in Carlyle vol. I**


Yet on 20 April 1653, Cromwell denounced and then dissolved the Rump Parliament, the purged remnant of the Long Parliament. What led him to this? Here is Cromwell's own explanation, taken from his opening speech to Barebone's Parliament:

**2.8**

We [ = the army leaders] did, with all faithfulness and sincerity, beseech them [ = the members of the Rump Parliament] that they would be mindful of their duty to God and men, in the discharge of the trust reposed in them . . . At last . . . the

Parliament men began to take the Act for a Representative to heart . . . But plainly
. . . that semblance of giving them a choice was only to recruit the House, the better     5
to perpetuate *themselves* . . . Finding that this spirit was not according to God; and
that the whole weight of this cause, which must needs be very dear unto us who had
so often adventured our lives for it . . . and seeing plainly that there was not here
any consideration to assert this cause and provide security for it, but only to cross
the troublesome people of the army . . . Truly, I say, when we saw all this, having     10
power in our hands, we could not resolve to let such monstrous proceedings go on,
and so to throw away all our liberties into the hands of those whom we had fought
against . . . to deliver them sluggishly up would render us the basest persons in the
world, and worthy to be accounted haters of God and His People. When it pleased
God to lay this close to our hearts; and indeed to show us that . . . His Cause . . .     15
would also in every point go to the ground, indeed this did add more considerations
to us, that there was a duty incumbent upon us.

**Cromwell to Barebone's Parliament, 4 July 1653, in Carlyle vol. II**

However, Dorothy Osborne expressed the reservations of many contemporaries when she wrote on 23 April 1653:

**2.9**

Bless me, what will become of us all now? Is not this a strange turn? . . . Well, 'tis a
pleasant world this. If Mr Pym were alive again I wonder what he would think of
these proceedings, and whether this would appear as great a breach of the privilege
of Parliament as the demanding [of] the five members.

*The Letters of Dorothy Osborne to William Temple*, ed. G.C. Moore Smith,
23 April 1653 (Oxford, 1928)

Nevertheless, for the rest of his career Cromwell tried to work with Parliaments. In July 1653 he summoned Barebone's Parliament [3.6 and 4.8], an
assembly of 140 men chosen for their godly religious views – people, as
Cromwell put it, with 'the root of the matter in them'. But this Parliament
dissolved itself on 12 December. *The Instrument of Government* (16 December
1653) made Cromwell Lord Protector and stipulated that a Parliament (known
as the first Protectorate Parliament) should meet on 3 September 1654. **2.10** is
taken from Cromwell's speech to this Parliament on 22 January 1655:

**2.10**

What hath happened since that time[1] I have not taken public notice of as declining
to entrench on Parliament['s] privileges. For sure I am you will all bear me witness,
that from your entering into the House . . . to this very day, you have had no

manner of interruption or hindrance of mine in proceeding to that blessed issue [that] the heart of a good man could propose to himself, to this very day. You see      5
you have me very much locked up, as to what you have transacted among
yourselves, from that time to this . . . I have been careful of your safety, and the
safety of those you represent, to whom I reckon myself a servant. But what
messages have I disturbed you withal? What injury or indignity hath been done, or
offered, either to your persons or to any privileges of Parliament, since you sat? I      10
looked at myself as strictly obliged by my oath . . . to give you all possible security,
and to keep you from any unparliamentary interruption . . . I say, I have been
caring for you, for your quiet sitting, caring for your privileges, as I said before, that
they might not be interrupted . . . I did think it to be my business rather to see the
utmost issue, and what God would produce by you, than unseasonably to      15
intermeddle with you.

¹ 'that time' = the assembly of the first Protectorate Parliament, 3 September 1654.

**Cromwell to the first Protectorate Parliament, 22 January 1655, in Carlyle
vol. II**

At the end of this speech, Cromwell dissolved the first Protectorate Parliament
[3.8]. However, a second Protectorate Parliament met on 17 September 1656.
The first session was prorogued on 26 June 1657; in 2.11 the Venetian Resident
describes Cromwell's opening of the second session.

**2.11**

On Wednesday [20 January 1658] in the morning Parliament was reopened, after a
recess of several months. The Upper House¹ also assembled, to which the Protector
betook himself. Arrived there he took his place under a superb canopy, all the lords
and judges being arranged there according to the ancient custom of that house. The
members of the lower chamber also went there and his Highness delivered to them a      5
short and eloquent speech upon the internal affairs of these realms . . . He
proceeded from Whitehall to Westminster by water and thence by coach to the
palace in great pomp. Other of his coaches followed and some magnificent led
horses, adorned with superb saddles and cloths, majestic for the gold and jewels
they contained, as well as the usual guards on horse and foot.

¹ 'The Upper House': as stipulated by *The Humble Petition and Advice*, the second
Protectorate Parliament consisted of the House of Commons and the 'Other House'.

**Francesco Giavarina, Venetian Resident in England, to the Doge and
Senate of Venice, 1 February 1658, in *Calendar of State Papers Venetian*,
ed. A.B. Hinds, vol. XXXI (1657–9)**

## Questions

1 Can Cromwell have been sincere in *both* 2.7 *and* 2.8? Give reasons for your answer.
2 Do 2.7 and 2.8 enable you to explain why Cromwell dissolved the Rump Parliament? Explain your answer.
3 To what extent do you think that the sentiments in 2.9 were justified?
4 How convincing do you find Cromwell's words in 2.10? Does the fact that he dissolved the first Protectorate Parliament at the end of this speech affect your answer?
5 What light does 2.11 shed on Cromwell's attitude to Parliament?
6 'A steady drift back towards the restoration of monarchy'. Discuss this view of the 1650s with reference to 2.8–2.11.

We now turn to one of the most puzzling aspects of Oliver Cromwell: his attitudes towards the kingship. It was perhaps the supreme irony of Cromwell's career that the man who had led the fight against Charles I should ultimately himself be offered the Crown. The documents in the next section [2.12–2.16] all relate to this paradox. 2.12 is drawn from a conversation on 27 September 1651 (shortly after Cromwell's victory at the battle of Worcester on 3 September) between Hermann Mylius, envoy of the small German principality of Oldenburg, and John Dury, librarian at St James's Palace. A year later, the common lawyer Bulstrode Whitelocke recorded a meeting with Cromwell in which the latter pondered the question of kingship [2.13]. Then follow two accounts by foreign observers. In 2.14 the Swedish envoy, Peter Julius Coyet, weighs up the pros and cons of Cromwell's assuming the kingship; while in 2.15 the Venetian ambassador in France reports how the English ambassador explained Cromwell's refusal of the Crown. Finally, there is an extract from the speech of 13 April 1657 in which Cromwell declined to become king [2.16]. For another extract from this speech, giving further reasons, see document 3.9.

2.12

[Dury:] Things will shortly happen which have been unheard of, and above all would open the eyes of those who live under kings and other sovereigns, and lead to great changes. General Cromwell's prudence, gallantry and good fortune prevail.
Mylius: Perhaps they will make him a Doge in the Commonwealth, like the Venetians and the Genoese . . . and confer that dignity on him by hereditary right to 5 continue in his descendants.

Dury: On this he cannot verify anything definite. [Cromwell] alone holds the
direction of political and military affairs in his hands. He is one who is worth all the
others put together, and, in effect, King.

**L. Miller,** *John Milton and the Oldenburg Safeguard* (Loewenthal Press,
New York, 1985)

**2.13**

What if a man should take upon him to be king? . . . I have heard some of your
profession [ = common lawyers] observe, that he who is actually king, whether by
election or descent, yet being once king, all acts done by him as king are lawful and
justifiable, as by any king who hath the crown by inheritance from his forefathers;
and that by an act of parliament in Henry VII's time, it is safer for those who act          5
under a king (be his title what it will) than for those who act under any other power.
And surely the power of a king is so great and high, and so universally understood
and reverenced by the people of this nation, that the title of it might not only
indemnify in a great measure those that act under it, but likewise be of great use and
advantage in such times as these, to curb the insolences and extravagances of those        10
whom the present powers cannot control, or at least are the persons themselves who
are thus insolent.

**Bulstrode Whitelocke,** *Memorials of the English Affairs*, vol. III (Oxford, 1853)

**2.14**

The longer the lord protector sits in the saddle, the securer his seat in it; so that
there is every likelihood that his government may last for the remainder of his life:
indeed, all circumstances lead me to believe that he will either try to get the law
altered by consent, or (which seems more probable) that he will very shortly assume
the title of king. There are indeed reasons which might seem to hinder such a step.       5
First . . . he would to a great extent alienate himself from the militia [ = the army],
and among them some high officers – such as General Lambert[1] and others like him
. . . to say nothing of the anabaptists,[2] who can neither wish nor suffer that the
government remain in one family. 2. The struggle between the nation . . . and the
royal family of Stuart . . . would . . . be transformed into a private quarrel between      10
the Houses of Cromwell and Stuart; and in that quarrel many would defect from the
protector. 3. . . . An Act of Parliament . . . lays it down that all kingly power in one
person is . . . abrogated for ever in England. But on the other hand there are other
and more powerful reasons to persuade him to the assumption of the royal title.
First, that this country has always been accustomed to be ruled by a king, and all          15
their English statutes and ancient laws are founded on that . . . 3. It is easier for the
protector to make himself king now than it was to become protector. 4. The nobility
. . . would be better satisfied; their pre-eminence and preservation, as experience has
taught, consisting solely in a kingly government. 5. General Lambert and his
followers could . . . be given such favours as to content him . . . 6. The anabaptists     20

. . . were not able to prevent the protector from attaining to his present exalted position, though it conflicts with their maxims no less than does the royal style and dignity . . . 8. The greater part of the country would be obliged in their own interests to stand by him . . . 9. All those in this country who have either supported the parliament against the king, or been neutral, have nothing to look for from a          25
Stuart restoration . . . 10. . . . The country . . . [feels] it to be a matter of indifference to them by whom they are ruled, if only they be preserved in the free enjoyment of their law and religion.

¹ 'General Lambert' = John Lambert, Parliamentarian general, author of *The Instrument of Government*, and later an opponent of *The Humble Petition and Advice*.
² 'anabaptists' = religious sect believing that only those baptised as adults can achieve salvation.

**Peter Julius Coyet, Swedish envoy, to King Charles X of Sweden, 1 June 1655, in *Swedish Diplomats at Cromwell's Court, 1655–6*, ed. M. Roberts (Camden Society, fourth series, vol. XXXVI, 1988)**


**2.15**

I have paid my respects to the house of Cromwell's ambassador, when we exchanged compliments. Afterwards he spoke of the Parliament of England. He said they wanted his master to take the title of King, but he seemed reluctant to do this since he wields more authority in his present position than he would as King, because he would be obliged to concede and renew many privileges and jurisdictions   5
to Parliament such as were granted by Henry VIII.

**Francesco Giustiniani, Venetian ambassador in France, to the Doge and Senate of Venice, 27 March 1657, in *Calendar of State Papers Venetian*, ed. A.B. Hinds, vol. XXXI (1657–9)**


**2.16**

[The Kingship] is not (I should say) so interwoven in the laws but that the laws may still be executed to equal justice, and equal satisfaction of the people, and equally to answer all objections as well without it as with it . . . Truly though the kingship be not a mere title but a name of office that runs through the whole of the law, yet it is not so *ratione nominis*, from the reason of the name, but from what is signified. It is   5
a name of office plainly implying the supreme authority . . . As such a title hath been fixed, so it may be unfixed . . . And certainly they, the primary legislative authority, had the disposal of it, and might have had it, and might have detracted from it, or changed it, and . . . so may you. And if it be so that you may, why then I say there is nothing of necessity in your argument, but all turns on consideration of   10
the expedience of it.

**Cromwell to the representatives of the second Protectorate Parliament, 13 April 1657, in Carlyle vol. III**

## Questions

1 What can be gleaned from **2.12** about Cromwell's position in the autumn of 1651?

2 **2.13** was written during the 1660s. What problems does this pose for its use as evidence of Cromwell's opinions in 1652?

3 Do you agree with the Swedish envoy that the reasons for Cromwell's becoming king were stronger than those against [**2.14**]? Why?

4 Comment on the reliability of **2.15** as evidence of Cromwell's motives.

5 How persuasive do you find Cromwell's arguments in **2.16**? Justify your answer.

6 To what extent do **2.12–2.16** enable you to explain why Cromwell refused the Crown?

We have already seen that a number of Cromwell's contemporaries viewed his political actions unfavourably [**2.6; 2.9**]. The following documents [**2.17–2.19**] explore further the reasons for this hostility. Their authors came from very different backgrounds. **2.17** is drawn from *The World's Mistake in Oliver Cromwell*, published in 1668 by the republican Slingsby Bethel. (For further extracts from this work, see documents **4.20** and **5.26**.) **2.18** was written in the 1660s by the widow of John Hutchinson, a Parliamentarian colonel and member of Parliament who retired from public life after Cromwell dissolved the Rump. **2.19** is an extract from the *Memoirs* of Edmund Ludlow, a former Parliamentarian general and member of the Long Parliament who turned against Cromwell after the dissolution of the Rump. Ludlow composed his *Memoirs* in exile during the 1660s and 1670s. (For another extract from this work, see **5.25**.)

### 2.17

[Cromwell's] want of honour, so well as honesty, appears yet further in that having, by a long series of seeming pious deportment, gained by his dissimulation good thoughts in his masters, the Long Parliament, and by his spiritual gifts winded [ = wound] himself into so good an opinion with his soldiers . . . that he could impose . . . what belief he pleased upon them, he made use of the credit he had with    5 each to abuse both, by many vile practices, for making himself popular, and the Parliament and army odious to one another; and because the artifices he used are too

many to innumerate, I shall but instance [a] . . . few, [such] as . . . his obstructing
the House in their business by long drawling speeches and other ways, and then
complaining of them to his soldiers that he could not get them to do anything that 10
was good; his giving fair words to everyone, without keeping promise with any,
except for his own advantage . . . and his deserting his Major-Generals . . . crying
out against them himself when he only had set them at work . . . What he did . . .
being for his own singular advancement . . . is unpardonable, and leaves him a
person to be truly admired for nothing but apostasy and ambition, and exceeding 15
Tiberius[1] in dissimulation.

[1] 'Tiberius' = a Roman emperor and notorious tyrant.

**Slingsby Bethel,** *The World's Mistake in Oliver Cromwell* **(London, 1668)**

### 2.18

Cromwell and his army grew wanton with their power, and invented a thousand
tricks of government which, when nobody opposed, they themselves fell to dislike
and vary every day . . . He makes up several sorts of mock parliaments, but not
finding one of them absolutely for his turn, turned them off again . . . True religion
was now almost lost, even among the religious party, and hypocrisy became an 5
epidemical disease . . . He at last exercised such an arbitrary power that the whole
land grew weary of him.

*Memoirs of the Life of Colonel Hutchinson . . . Written by his Widow Lucy,*
ed. J. Hutchinson (London, 1806)

### 2.19

Colonel Sadler[1] said . . . that he was confident the difference between Cromwell and
me was grounded upon mistakes, he having heard him express great affection to me,
with protestations that he wished me as well as any man in the three nations. I
thought it not convenient to take much pains to undeceive him [= Sadler], but was
rather willing he should believe that he [= Cromwell] spoke in earnest, tho[ugh] 5
indeed he loved no person living any farther than he served to promote his
ambition; for how could it be expected that one who had sacrificed his conscience
and honour, as well as the cause of his country, to the idol of his pride, should
scruple to trample under foot any man that stood in his way?

[1] 'Colonel Sadler' = Thomas Sadler, colonel of infantry in Ireland.

*The Memoirs of Edmund Ludlow,* ed. C.H. Firth, vol. I (Oxford, 1894)

## Questions

1  Are **2.17–2.19** largely expressing similar criticisms of Cromwell or different ones? Explain your answer.

2  What evidence *for* and *against* the views in **2.17–2.19** have you encountered earlier in this chapter, and elsewhere?

3  Though their authors all lived through the 1650s, **2.17–2.19** were all written *after* Cromwell's death. Does this affect their reliability as evidence of how Cromwell was perceived by his contemporaries?

The final section of this chapter [**2.20–2.26**] is devoted to contemporary images and depictions of Cromwell. We begin by comparing the coins minted during the Interregnum with those issued under Charles I. **2.20** appeared in 1631–2. **2.21** and **2.22** both date from the 1650s and reveal the different designs of coins before [**2.21**] and after [**2.22**] Cromwell became Lord Protector. In the days before photographs, the cinema or television, these would have been the images of Cromwell with which most people would have been familiar.

**2.20**

A                      B

The inscriptions read:

(A)  CAROLVS D.G. MAG. BRIT. FR. ET HIB. REX [Charles, by the grace of God, King of Great Britain, France and Ireland]

(B)  CVLTORES SVI DEVS PROTEGIT [God protects his worshippers]

**Charles I gold crown, viewed on both sides, 1631–2, the Tower Mint, London; in the Ashmolean Museum, Oxford**

2.21

A                                                          B

The inscriptions read:
(A)    THE COMMONWEALTH OF ENGLAND
(B)    GOD WITH VS

Commonwealth shilling, viewed on both sides, 1652, the Tower Mint,
London; in the British Museum

2.22

A                                                          B

The inscriptions read:
(A)    OLIVAR D.G. RP. ANG. SCO. ET HIB. &c. PRO. [Oliver, by the grace of
         God, Protector of the Republic of England, Scotland and Ireland etc.]
(B)    PAX QVAERITVR BELLO [Peace is sought by War]

Oliver Cromwell half-crown, viewed on both sides, 1656, the Tower Mint,
London; in the British Museum

The design on the Great Seal of England, which was used to seal all major government documents, was rather different. **2.23** shows both sides of the Great Seal made in 1651:

**2.23**

A

B

The inscriptions read:
(A)  THE GREAT SEAL OF
      ENGLAND 1651
(B)  THE THIRD YEARE OF
      FREEDOME BY GOD'S
      BLESSING RESTORED

**The Great Seal of England, viewed on both sides, 1651; in the Mansell Collection**

Many official pamphlets also contained images of Cromwell, and these often depicted him as an heroic military leader. **2.24** is taken from *A Perfect Table of One Hundred Forty and Five Victories Obtained by the Lord Lieutenant of Ireland*, published in 1650.

2.24

*A Perfect Table of One Hundred Forty and Five Victories Obtained by the Lord Lieutenant of Ireland*, title page (London, 1650)

Engravings such as 2.24 were usually printed (or at least inspired) by the government. But Cromwell's opponents often depicted him in much less flattering terms. For example, 'The Royall Oake of Brittayne' [2.25] is taken from Clement Walker's *Anarchia Anglicana: or, the History of Independency. The Second Part* (1649). Walker was the Parliamentarian MP for Wells (Somerset) from 1646. He always hoped to reach a settlement with Charles, and was among the MPs 'purged' by Colonel Pride in December 1648. *Anarchia Anglicana* blamed Cromwell for the regicide, and this cartoon shows him ordering 'the royall oake' to be axed. Its publication led to Walker's imprisonment in the Tower in November 1649.

2.25

'The Royall Oake of Brittayne', in Clement Walker, *Anarchia Anglicana: or, the History of Independency. The Second Part* (London, 1649)

Some inhabitants of the Dutch Republic were especially scathing about Cromwell. In particular, they mocked his flirtation with the Crown and his obsession (as they saw it) with England's commercial interests. Both concerns are illustrated in a Dutch satire entitled 'The Horrible Tail Man' [**2.26**]. Cromwell is being offered the Crown, while Dutch, Irish, Scots and Royalists cut off sections of his tail, filled with money.

**2.26**

'The Horrible Tail Man', a Dutch satire; in the British Museum

## Questions

1 Explain and comment on the differences between **2.20–2.22** with regard to:
  (i) the inscriptions
  (ii) the images.
2 Do **2.20–2.22** affect your answer to question 6, page 37? Explain your response.
3 What can be learnt from **2.23** about the values and policies of the English government in 1651?
4 Is the depiction of Cromwell in **2.24** consistent or inconsistent with the impression of him which emerges from **2.21–2.23**? Explain your answer.

5   Look at **2.25** and explain the significance of the following:
     (i) the words coming from Cromwell's mouth
    (ii) the words coming from the axemen's mouths
   (iii) the books hanging from 'the royall oake':
        (a)  *The Eikon Basilike*
        (b)  *The Bible*
        (c)  *Magna Carta*
        (d)  *Statutes*
        (e)  *[Law] Reports*
    (iv) the thunderstorms raging above Cromwell's head
     (v) the pigs 'fatted for slaughter' in the foreground.
6   What message about Cromwell is conveyed in **2.26**? Does the inset (top left-hand corner) help you to explain this? Justify your response.
7   How far do **2.20–2.26** confirm or conflict with the views of Cromwell which you have formed earlier in this chapter? Explain your answer.
8   'A political opportunist, driven primarily by ambition and self-interest.' Discuss and debate this view of Cromwell, using evidence from this chapter.

# 3 Cromwell's religious attitudes

In Britain today, there is no necessary link between someone's political opinions and their religious beliefs. Membership of a certain church (or no church) does not imply that an individual will vote for a particular party in a General Election. But much recent research has suggested that in seventeenth-century Britain, religion and politics were far more closely related. They should be seen not as watertight compartments, but as integral parts of a single world-view. Thus, royal absolutism was often associated with Catholicism, while Parliament was seen as the guardian of Protestantism. Religious beliefs sometimes had a direct impact on how people behaved politically: Dr John Morrill has even argued that the most appropriate label for the English Civil Wars is 'the last of the Wars of Religion'. In exploring Cromwell's complex life and career, it is therefore fundamental to explore his religious beliefs, although you must decide for yourself just how much they explain. The documents in this chapter try to elucidate two questions: what was the nature of Cromwell's religion; and how far did it determine his actions both as a soldier and as a politician? We will look particularly at some of his letters and speeches, at both public and private utterances, and also at the views of contemporaries who sometimes refused to take Cromwell at face-value.

Cromwell's early religious development is very difficult to reconstruct. For many years historians believed that he had been influenced by puritanism from an early age. Although 'puritanism' is a highly complex term, covering a variety of different beliefs, it remains useful as a general label for those people who disliked the traces of Catholicism in the late Tudor and early Stuart Church (such as Bishops, vestments, and the Prayer Book), and who felt that the English Reformation was still incomplete. It used to be thought that Cromwell's schoolmaster at Huntingdon Grammar School, Thomas Beard, held such views and that (like many puritans) he believed that God made himself visible in this world through 'providences'. His book *The Theatre of God's Judgements* (1597) was interpreted as a list of cases in which God had intervened in human affairs to punish sinners. But this view of Beard has recently been challenged by Dr Morrill (see the Bibliography). No longer can we assume that

Beard was a devout puritan or that he shaped Cromwell's religious attitudes. It is also unclear whether the strongly puritan atmosphere of Sidney Sussex College, Cambridge – where Cromwell studied for about a year in 1616–17 – had any direct influence upon him. Before 1640, there are only fragmentary clues to the nature of Cromwell's religious beliefs. Easily the most important sources are two letters of January 1636 and October 1638 [3.1 and 3.2]. Document 3.1 comes from Cromwell's earliest surviving letter, written on behalf of a puritan preacher faced with the loss of his livelihood. 3.2 is taken from a letter to Mrs St John, wife of Cromwell's cousin and political ally, the radical MP Oliver St John.

### 3.1

Mr Storie: Amongst the catalogue of those good works which your fellow citizens and other countrymen have done, this will not be reckoned for the least, that they have provided for the feeding of souls . . . Such a work as this was your erecting the lecture [ = post for a preacher] in our country [ = county] in . . . which you placed Dr Welles, a man for goodness and industry and ability to do good every way: not   5 short of any I know in England, and I am persuaded that since his coming the Lord by him hath wrought much good amongst us . . . It were a piteous thing to see a lecture fall . . . in these times wherein we see they are suppressed with too much haste and violence by the enemies of God's truth . . . I beseech you therefore in the bowels of Christ Jesus, put it forward, and let the good man have his pay. The souls   10 of God's children will bless you for it.

**Cromwell to Mr Storie, 11 January 1636, in Carlyle vol. I**

### 3.2

Yet to honour my God by declaring what He hath done for my soul, in this I am confident, and I will be so. Truly, then, this I find: that He giveth springs in a dry and barren wilderness where no water is . . . My soul is with the congregation of the firstborn, my body rests in hope, and if here I may honour my God either by doing or by suffering, I shall be most glad. Truly no poor creature hath more cause to put   5 forth himself in the cause of his God than I. I have had plentiful wages beforehand, and I am sure I shall never earn the least mite. The Lord accept me in His Son, and give us to walk in the light, as He is the light. He it is that enlighteneth our blackness, our darkness . . . One beam in a dark place hath exceeding much refreshment in it: blessed be His name for shining upon so dark a heart as mine!   10 You know what my manner of life hath been. Oh, I lived in and loved darkness, and hated the light; I was a chief, the chief of sinners. This is true: I hated godliness, yet God had mercy on me. O the riches of His mercy. Praise Him for me, that He who hath begun a good work would perfect it to the day of Christ.

**Cromwell to Mrs St John, 13 October 1638, in Carlyle vol. I**

## Questions

1  What do you think Cromwell means by the following phrases:
   (i) 'the enemies of God's truth' [3.1, line 9]
   (ii) 'the congregation of the firstborn' [3.2, lines 3–4]?
2  In your wider reading, have you found any evidence which confirms or conflicts with Cromwell's statement that he had once been 'the chief of sinners' [3.2, line 12]?
3  In what ways do 3.1 and 3.2 illuminate our understanding of Cromwell's religious beliefs, and of how he came to hold them?
4  How far do 3.1 and 3.2 help us to explain why Cromwell took up arms for Parliament in the summer of 1642?

During the years 1642–51, Cromwell established himself as a brilliant military commander. Through the first and second Civil Wars, to the conquests of Ireland and Scotland, his run of success was unbroken. How far was it religion that drove Cromwell on? Did he see himself as engaged in some kind of crusade? Certainly Cromwell's reaction to the events of this period tells us much about his religious beliefs. His letters referred constantly to 'providences', to occasions (especially during battles) when God was clearly visible in the world. He seems to have felt God's presence with him, and his first response to any victory was to give all the credit to God. This is apparent in document 3.3, a letter written after the battle of Marston Moor to Cromwell's brother-in-law, Colonel Valentine Walton. This is also a letter of condolence, for Walton's son (Cromwell's nephew) had been killed in the battle. Cromwell's advice to his bereaved relative is a moving expression of his personal faith.

### 3.3

Truly England and the Church of God hath had a great favour from the Lord, in this great victory given unto us . . . It had all the evidences of an absolute victory obtained by the Lord's blessing upon the godly party principally. We never charged but we routed the enemy . . . God made them as stubble to our swords, we charged their regiments of foot with our horse, routed all we charged . . . Give glory, all the    5
glory, to God. Sir, God hath taken away your eldest son by a cannon-shot . . . Sir, you know my trials this way:[1] but the Lord supported me with this, that the Lord took him into the happiness we all pant after and live for. There is your precious child full of glory, to know [neither] sin nor sorrow any more . . . He was a precious young man, fit for God. You have cause to bless the Lord. He is a glorious saint in    10
Heaven, wherein you ought exceedingly to rejoice. Let this drink up your sorrow; seeing these are not feigned words to comfort you, but the thing is so real and

undoubted a truth. You may do all things by the strength of Christ. Seek that, and you shall easily bear your trial. Let this public mercy to the Church of God make you . . . forget your private sorrow. The Lord be your strength.

¹ Cromwell's son Oliver had died of smallpox in the spring of 1644.

**Cromwell to Colonel Valentine Walton, 5 July 1644, in Carlyle vol. I**

However, it was one thing to believe that God was visible in military and political events; it was quite another to interpret these signs and to perceive their true significance. People were worldly, imperfect creatures, all too ready to ignore or misinterpret God's will. This is the theme of Cromwell's letter [3.4] to his cousin, Colonel Robert Hammond, Governor of the Isle of Wight, dated 25 November 1648:

### 3.4

As to outward dispensations, if we may so call them, we have not been without our share of beholding some remarkable providences, and appearances of the Lord. His presence hath been amongst us, and by the light of His countenance we have prevailed . . . If thou wilt seek, seek to know the mind of God in all that chain of Providence, whereby God brought thee thither, and that person to thee; how, before   5
and since, God has ordered him, and affairs concerning him: and then tell me, whether there be not some glorious and high meaning in all this, above what thou hast yet attained? And, laying aside thy fleshly reason, seek of the Lord to teach thee what that is; and He will do it . . . My dear friend, let us look into providences; surely they mean somewhat. They hang so together; have been so constant, so clear   10
and unclouded.

**Cromwell to Colonel Robert Hammond, 25 November 1648, in Carlyle vol. I**

If it was man's task to interpret God's will and then implement it, it is not surprising that Cromwell often hesitated until he was sure what God wanted. For instance, he vacillated for months over whether or not to put Charles I on trial and execute him. But when he finally became convinced that this was a king 'against whom the Lord has witnessed', he demanded that 'we cut off his head with the Crown upon it'. If we believe his own rhetoric, Cromwell saw himself as a kind of blank sheet of paper on which God could write his instructions. He could therefore find himself doing things which he had never anticipated. Here, for example, is his account [3.5] of the massacre at Wexford on 11 October 1649:

3.5

We [were] intending better to this place [Wexford] than so great a ruin, hoping the town might be of more use to you and your army, yet God would not have it so; but, by an unexpected providence, in His righteous justice, brought a just judgment upon them; causing them to become a prey to the soldier, who by their piracies had made preys of so many families, and made with their bloods to answer the cruelties   5 which they had exercised upon the lives of divers poor Protestants . . . Thus it hath pleased God to give into your hands this other mercy, for which, as for all, we pray God may have all the glory. Indeed, your instruments are poor and weak, and can do nothing but through believing, and that is the gift of God also.

**Cromwell to William Lenthall, Speaker of the House of Commons, 11 October 1649, in Carlyle vol. I**

## Questions

1 Document 3.3 reveals 'in its tenderness and sympathy, its enthusiasm and its devotion to the cause, the depths of Cromwell's nature, and the secret of his power over his comrades in arms' (C.H. Firth, *Oliver Cromwell and the Rule of the Puritans in England*). Discuss.

2 What do you think Cromwell is referring to in the phrase 'some remarkable providences, and appearances of the Lord' [3.4, line 2]?

3 Who is 'that person' [3.4, line 5]? What seems to have been Cromwell's attitude towards him at this time and why?

4 What event is referred to in 3.5, lines 4–6?

5 How convincing do you find Cromwell's argument in 3.5? How far can it justify the massacre at Wexford?

6 Do 3.3–3.5 suggest that Cromwell's approach to the events of the 1640s was consistent, or that it changed over time? Justify your response.

7 Using the evidence presented in 3.3–3.5, and your wider reading, how far do you think Cromwell's actions during the Civil Wars were motivated by a belief in God's Providence?

It never occurred to Cromwell that he had any choice but to obey God's will as expressed in 'providences'. To conform was absolutely 'necessary', and Cromwell often associated the two words 'providence' and 'necessity' very closely together. This link emerges in the next four documents [3.6–3.9], which are all taken from speeches delivered between July 1653 and April 1657. We begin with Cromwell's opening address to Barebone's Parliament on 4 July 1653 [3.6].

**3.6**

Truly God hath called you to this work by, I think, as wonderful providences as ever passed upon the sons of men in so short a time. And truly I think, taking the argument of necessity, for the government must not fall; taking the appearance of the hand of God in this thing, I am sure you would have been loath it should have been resigned into the hands of wicked men and enemies! I am sure, God would not 5 have it so. It's come, therefore, to you by the way of necessity; by the wise Providence of God . . . God hath owned you in the eyes of the world; and thus, by coming hither, you own Him . . . Consider the circumstances by which you are called hither; through what strivings, through what blood you are come hither, where neither you, nor I, nor any man living, three months ago, had a thought to 10 have seen such a company taking upon them, or rather being called to take, the supreme authority of this nation! Therefore, own your call! . . . [Barebone's Parliament is] of God! And it hath been unprotected, unthought of by you and us. And indeed it hath been the way God hath dealt with us all along, to keep things from our eyes, so that we have seen nothing, in all His dispensations, long 15 beforehand: which is also a witness, in some measure, to our integrity.

**Cromwell to Barebone's Parliament, 4 July 1653, in Carlyle vol. II**

Yet within six months, Barebone's Parliament had dissolved itself amid much bitterness. This was typical of the years that followed: the 1650s saw a series of unsuccessful attempts to create new institutions of government to fill the vacuum caused by the regicide. But Cromwell accepted such difficulties as the inevitable fate of a 'chosen people'. He was convinced that there was a direct parallel between the experience of the Israelites described in the Old Testament and that of the English in the mid-seventeenth century. Under Charles I, the English had been in bondage, like the Israelites in Egypt. But with the regicide they had broken free, in a way as dramatic as the crossing of the Red Sea. Now they were in the desert, searching for the Promised Land, guided by a 'pillar of fire' in the form of God's 'providences'. Cromwell saw himself in the role of Moses, leading a confused and often reluctant people. He warmly welcomed each new Parliament during the 1650s, hoping that it would bring England nearer to the Promised Land, but was always disappointed. Documents 3.7 and 3.8 represent a case study of Cromwell's approach to the first Protectorate Parliament, which sat between 4 September 1654 and 22 January 1655. His opening address [3.7] was very optimistic, and drew out the parallels with the Old Testament quite explicitly:

### 3.7

After so many changes and turnings, which this nation hath laboured under, to have
such a day of hope as this is, and such a door of hope opened by God to us, truly I
believe, some months since, would have been above all our thoughts! . . . Yet these
are but entrances and doors of hope, wherein, through the blessing of God, you may
enter into rest and peace. But you are not yet entered! You were told, today, of a     5
people brought out of Egypt towards the land of Canaan; but through unbelief,
murmuring, repining, and other temptations and sins wherewith God was provoked,
they were fain to come back again, and linger many years in the wilderness before
they came to the place of rest. We are thus far, through the mercy of God. We have
cause to take notice of it, that we are not brought into misery, not totally wrecked;     10
but have, as I said before, a door of hope open. And I may say this to you: if the
Lord's blessing and His presence go along with the management of affairs at this
meeting, you will be enabled to put the topstone to this work, and make the nation
happy. But this must be by knowing the true state of affairs; that you are yet, like
the people under circumcision, but raw . . . And therefore I wish that you may go     15
forward, and not backward; and in brief that you may have the blessings of God
upon your endeavours! It's one of the great ends of calling this Parliament, that this
Ship of the Commonwealth may be brought into a safe harbour; which, I assure
you, it will not well be, without your counsel and advice. You have great works
upon your hands.

**Cromwell to the first Protectorate Parliament, 4 September 1654, in Carlyle
vol. II**

Yet only five months later, Cromwell used almost identical language to justify
the dissolution of this Parliament at the earliest possible opportunity. Inevitably this provoked charges of inconsistency and self-interest. Some of
Cromwell's contemporaries felt that he used 'providence' and 'necessity' –
which were, after all, open to a variety of interpretations – to conceal his own
ambition and ruthlessness (see **3.20–3.23**). The first part of Cromwell's speech
on 22 January 1655 [**3.8**] contains his answer to these charges, while the
concluding section gives his reasons for dissolving the Parliament.

### 3.8

I must tell you this: that as I undertook this government in the simplicity of my
heart and as before God, and to do the part of an honest man, and to be true to the
interest which in my conscience I think is dear to many of you . . . so I can say that
no particular interest, either of myself, estate, honour, or family, are, or have been,
prevalent with me to this undertaking . . . But if any man shall object, 'It is an easy     5
thing to talk of necessities when men create necessities: would not the Lord
Protector make himself great and his family great? Doth not he make these

necessities? And then he will come upon the people with this argument of
necessity!', this were something hard indeed. But I have not known what it is to
make necessities, whatsoever the judgments or thoughts of men are. And I say this,     10
not only to this Assembly, but to the world, that man liveth not that can come to me
and charge me with having, in these great revolutions, made necessities. I challenge
even all that fear God . . . All these things have been the wise disposings of the
Almighty; though instruments have had their passions and frailties. And I think it is
an honour to God to acknowledge the necessities to have been of God's imposing,     15
when truly they have been so . . . The Lord hath poured this nation from vessel to
vessel, till He poured it into your lap . . . I am confident it came so into your hands
. . . by Divine Providence and Dispensation . . . The Lord hath done such things
amongst us as have not been known in the world these thousand years, and yet
notwithstanding is not owned by us! . . . I think myself bound – it is my duty to     20
God and the people of these nations, to their safety and good in every respect – I
think it my duty to tell you that it is not for the profit of these nations, nor fit for the
common and public good, for you to continue here any longer. And therefore I do
declare unto you, that I do dissolve this Parliament.

**Cromwell to the first Protectorate Parliament, 22 January 1655, in Carlyle
vol. II**

## Questions

1   Explain and comment on the following phrases:
   (i) 'a people brought out of Egypt towards the land of Canaan' [3.7, **lines
       5–6**]
   (ii) 'like the people under circumcision, but raw' [3.7, **lines 14–15**].
2   In the light of 3.6 and 3.7, how far do you believe Cromwell's denial of self-
   interest in 3.8, **lines 3–10**?
3   'Turbid oratory, protestations of his own virtue and their [ = MPs']
   waywardness.' Do you agree with H.R. Trevor-Roper's view of 3.8?
   Explain your answer.
4   Put yourself in the position of a member of the first Protectorate
   Parliament. What would be your reaction to Cromwell's opening and
   closing addresses [3.7 and 3.8], and why?
5   Have you, in your wider reading, found any evidence which suggests that
   Cromwell had other reasons for dissolving the first Protectorate Parliament
   besides those expressed in 3.8?
6   'The reference to Providence was with Cromwell an infallible indication of
   a political change of front' (S.R. Gardiner, *History of the Great Civil War*,
   vol. IV). Do documents 3.6–3.8 bear this out?

This brings us back to one of the most controversial episodes in Cromwell's career: his rejection of Parliament's offer of the Crown in 1657. We have already examined Cromwell's attitudes towards the kingship in Chapter 2, but this particular episode also fits well into a chapter on his religious beliefs. The formal offer of the kingship was made in *The Humble Petition and Advice* on 23 February, yet it was not until mid-April that Cromwell finally declined it. We looked earlier [2.16] at an extract from Cromwell's speech to the committee of MPs sent to receive his final answer on the kingship. In another passage from this speech [3.9], Cromwell returned to the themes of 'providence' and 'necessity':

**3.9**

If your arguments come upon me to enforce upon me the ground of necessity, why, then I have no room to answer: for what must be, must be! And therefore I did reckon it much of my business to consider whether there were such a necessity, or would arise such a necessity, from those arguments . . . It is a question not of necessity; we have power to settle it as conveniency directs . . . Truly, the      5
Providence of God hath laid aside this title of King providentially *de facto*; . . . God hath seemed providentially, seemed to appear as a providence, not only to strike at the family but at the name . . . *De facto* it is blotted out . . . God hath seemed so to deal with the family that He blasted the very title . . . I will not seek to set up that, that Providence hath destroyed, and laid in the dust; and I would not build Jericho      10
again.

**Cromwell to the representatives of the second Protectorate Parliament, 13 April 1657, in Carlyle vol. III**

## Questions

1  How far are Cromwell's arguments in **3.9** consistent with those which he had expressed on previous occasions?

2  How does **3.9** affect your answer to questions 5 and 6 on page 40?

3  How effectively does **3.9** refute Henry Marten's charge that Cromwell was 'king-ridden' [**1.16**, line 2]?

4  How far do **3.6–3.9** support Blair Worden's comment that 'providentialism afforded infinite scope for self-deception' ('Providence and Politics in Cromwellian England')?

5  Documents 3.1–3.5 are all taken from private letters written between 1636
   and 1649; 3.6–3.9 are all taken from public speeches made between 1653
   and 1657. Looking back over these documents, consider the following:
   (i)  Did Cromwell's religious attitudes change over this period? If so,
        how?
   (ii) Did the influence of religion on his actions tend to increase or decrease,
        or neither?
   (iii) How consistent was Cromwell's public rhetoric with his private
        rhetoric? What does your answer suggest to you about his character?

In many of his beliefs, Cromwell can be described as an orthodox Calvinist.
That is to say, he believed that God had predestined some men and women to
be saved (the 'elect') and all others to be damned (the 'reprobate'). He was also
typical in his conviction that God made himself visible in human events
through 'providences'. Blair Worden has described providentialism as 'the
language of everyday Puritan belief'. But in one respect, Cromwell seems to
have been unusual. Most puritans assumed that God's 'elect' were contained
within the particular church to which they belonged – a belief which
discouraged toleration of others, who were assumed to be among the 'reprobate'. By contrast, Cromwell thought that the 'elect' were divided among the
different churches on earth, and that if these scattered fragments could only be
brought together, then a united, godly commonwealth would emerge. Cromwell's personal friends ranged from the former Anglican Archbishop of
Armagh, James Ussher, to the Quaker leader George Fox. He believed that
religious toleration was essential to achieve unity, and the next four documents
[3.10–3.14] all explore this distinctive theme in Cromwell's thought. We begin
with two extracts written in 1650. Document 3.10 is taken from Cromwell's
letter to the General Assembly of the (frequently intolerant) Scottish Kirk
(Church), on 3 August. 3.11 comes from a letter to the Governor of Edinburgh
Castle, written on 12 September.

### 3.10

Your own guilt is too much for you to bear: bring not therefore upon yourself the
blood of innocent men, deceived with pretences of King and Covenant, from whose
eyes you hide a better knowledge. I am persuaded that divers of you, who lead the
people, have laboured to build yourselves in these things wherein you have censured
others, and established yourselves upon the Word of God. Is it therefore infallibly    5
agreeable to the Word of God, all that you say? I beseech you, in the bowels of
Christ, think it possible you may be mistaken.

**Cromwell to the Commissioners of the General Assembly of the Scottish
Kirk, 3 August 1650, in Carlyle vol. II**

**3.11**

Your pretended fear lest error should step in, is like the man who would keep all the wine out [of] the country lest men should be drunk. It will be found an unjust and unwise jealousy, to deny a man the liberty he has by nature upon a supposition he may abuse it. When he doth abuse it, judge. If a man speak foolishly, ye suffer him gladly because ye are wise; if erroneously, the truth more appears by your                5 conviction. Stop such a man's mouth with sound words that cannot be gainsayed. If he speak blasphemously, or to the disturbance of the public peace, let the civil magistrate punish him: if truly, rejoice in the truth.

**Cromwell to the Governor of Edinburgh Castle, 12 September 1650, in Carlyle vol. II**

Cromwell made his lengthiest and most impassioned plea for religious toleration in a speech to the second Protectorate Parliament on 17 September 1656 [**3.12**]. He stressed that inner piety mattered far more than outward patterns of worship, and this distrust of external 'forms' of religion exactly parallels his claim that he was not 'wedded and glued to forms of government' (see Chapter 2, p. 31). Yet this tolerance inevitably conflicted with Cromwell's duty as Head of State to preserve law and order. Five months before, a Quaker, James Nayler, had re-enacted Christ's entry into Jerusalem on Palm Sunday by riding into Bristol on a donkey, with women throwing palms at his feet. Many MPs wished to punish him severely for blasphemy and anarchy, but Cromwell's influence ensured that the final sentence – even though it still included flogging, branding and tongue-boring – was rather more lenient. Cromwell was torn between his tolerant instincts and his duties as ruler: **3.12** shows how he tried to resolve this dilemma.

**3.12**

Our practice since the last Parliament hath been to let all this nation see that whatever pretensions to religion would continue quiet [and] peaceable . . . should enjoy conscience and liberty to themselves; and not make religion a pretence for arms and blood, truly we have suffered them, and that cheerfully, so to enjoy their own liberties. Whatsoever is contrary, and not peaceable, let the pretence be never          5 so specious – if it tend to combination, to interests and factions – we shall not care, by the grace of God, whom we meet withal, though never so specious, though never so quiet . . . truly I am against all liberty of conscience repugnant to this . . . That men that believe in Jesus Christ – that's the form that gives the being to true religion, faith in Christ and walking in a profession answerable to that faith – men          10 that believe the remission of sins through the blood of Christ and free justification by the blood of Christ, and live upon the grace of God: that those men that are certain they are so, they are members of Jesus Christ, and are to Him as the apple of

His eye. Whoever hath this faith, let his form be what it will, [if] he [is] walking
peaceably, without the prejudicing of others under another form, it is a debt due to    15
God and Christ . . . [that] that Christian may . . . enjoy this liberty. If a man of one
form will be trampling upon the heels of another form; if an Independent,[1] for
example, will despise him who is under Baptism,[2] and will revile him, and reproach
and provoke him, I will not suffer it in him. If, on the other side, those on the
Anabaptists' judgment shall be censuring the godly ministers of the nation that    20
profess . . . Independency; or those that profess under Presbytery,[3] shall be
reproaching or speaking evil of them, traducing and censuring them – as I would
not be willing to see the day on which England shall be in the power of the
Presbytery to impose upon the consciences of others that profess faith in Christ – so
I will not endure any to reproach them. But God give us hearts and spirits to keep    25
things equal.

[1] 'Independent' = someone opposed to a national Church, who believes that each
congregation should be independent.
[2] 'him who is under Baptism' = an Anabaptist: someone who believes that only those
baptised as adults can achieve salvation.
[3] 'Presbytery' = a national Church organised around local, provincial and national
assemblies, such as existed in Scotland.

**Cromwell to the second Protectorate Parliament, 17 September 1656, in
Carlyle vol. II**

Cromwell was also unusual among his contemporaries in extending his
tolerance to the Jews. The 1650s saw the first serious attempts to re-admit Jews
to England since the Middle Ages. In the autumn of 1655, the Leveller Richard
Overton told the former Royalist Sir Marmaduke Langdale:

**3.13**

I made enquiry into the conditions of the Jews . . . I find they are in conjunction
with Cromwell; some of the Rabbis are learning English on purpose to live in
England and must go speedily over. They have their meetings at London, and those
Rabbis are to be sent thither for that purpose, so that I am very glad I dealt with
them by proxy. Not one of them knows anything of me, or what my intentions were.  5
Had they, Cromwell should have known it.

**Richard Overton to Sir Marmaduke Langdale, 13 September 1655, in *The
Nicholas Papers*, ed. G.F. Warner, vol. III (Camden Society, second series,
vol. LVII, 1897)**

The final document in this sequence [3.14] is taken from a pamphlet written by
a radical army officer in 1652. It reports Cromwell's words at a meeting of the
Committee of the Army, and shows clearly the extent of his commitment to
religious toleration:

**3.14**

At a debate of the Honourable Committee [of the Army] . . . his Excellency [the Lord General, Oliver Cromwell] with much Christian zeal and affection for his own conscience professed also, that he had rather that Mahumetanism[1] were permitted amongst us, than that one of God's children should be persecuted.

[1] 'Mahumetanism' = Mohammedanism, or Islam, commonly seen in this period as the most terrible heresy of all.

**Roger Williams,** *The Fourth Paper, Presented by Maior Butler* (London, 1652)

## Questions

1 What do **3.10** and **3.12** tell us about Cromwell's attitude towards the Scottish Presbyterian Church? Might other considerations besides religion have shaped this attitude?

2 What limits does Cromwell set to 'liberty of conscience' in **3.12**? How far are these arguments consistent with those reported in **3.14**?

3 How does the date of **3.12** help us to explain its contents?

4 Documents **3.13–3.14** are the only ones in this chapter so far not taken from either Cromwell's letters or his speeches. Does this pose problems for their use as evidence of his opinions?

5 How does 'religious toleration' accurately describe what Cromwell is urging in **3.10–3.12** and **3.14**?

6 Using your wider reading, how far did Cromwell put the views expressed in **3.10–3.14** into action?

How far did Cromwell's ambitions extend to the creation of a 'godly nation'? The 1650s were notable for a series of attempts to improve the quality of preaching through careful vetting of the clergy. First of all, on 20 March 1654 'An Ordinance for Appointing Commissioners for Approbation of Publique Preachers' established a national body of 'triers' to examine rigorously all new clergy before allowing them to preach [**3.15**]. The ordinance stated:

**3.15**

Whereas for some time past hitherto there hath not been any certain course established for the supplying vacant places with able and fit persons to preach the Gospel, by reason whereof . . . many weak, scandalous, popish and ill-affected persons have intruded themselves, or been brought in, to the great grief and trouble

of the good people of this nation . . . Be it ordained . . . that every person . . . before 5
he be admitted into any such benefice or lecture, be judged and approved by the
persons hereafter named to be a person for the Grace of God in him, his holy and
unblameable conversation, as also for his knowledge and utterance, able and fit to
preach the Gospel.

**'An Ordinance for Appointing Commissioners for Approbation of Publique Preachers', 20 March 1654, in *Acts and Ordinances of the Interregnum, 1642–1660*, ed. C.H. Firth and R.S. Rait, vol. II (London, 1911)**

This was followed on 28 August 1654 by 'An Ordinance for Ejecting
Scandalous, Ignorant and Insufficient Ministers and Schoolmasters' [3.16].
This appointed commissioners in each county who were required to eject:

### 3.16

. . . such ministers and schoolmasters . . . as shall be proved guilty of holding or
maintaining . . . blasphemous and atheistical opinions . . . or guilty of profane
cursing or swearing, perjury, subornation [ = bribery] of perjury, such as shall hold,
teach or maintain . . . popish opinions . . . or be guilty of adultery, fornication,
drunkenness, common haunting of taverns or alehouses, frequent quarrelling or 5
fighting, frequent playing at cards or dice, profaning of the Sabbath day . . . such as
have . . . used the Common Prayer Book since 1 January last . . . or do encourage or
countenance by word or practice any Whitsun-ales,[1] wakes,[2] morris dances,
maypoles, stage plays, or such like licentious practices.

[1] 'ales' = festivals at which ale was drunk.
[2] 'wakes' = the vigils or eves before a festival.

**'An Ordinance for Ejecting Scandalous, Ignorant and Insufficient Ministers and Schoolmasters', 28 August 1654, in *Acts and Ordinances of the Interregnum, 1642–1660*, ed. C.H. Firth and R.S. Rait, vol. II (London, 1911)**

Three years later, in a speech to the representatives of the second Protectorate
Parliament [3.17], Cromwell reflected on the achievements of the 'triers' and
'ejectors':

### 3.17

Truly we have settled very much the business of the ministry . . . If I have anything
to rejoice in before the Lord in this world, as having done any good or service, I can
say it from my heart, and I know I say the truth, that it hath been this. Let any man

say what he will to the contrary, he will give me leave to enjoy my own opinion in it, and my own conscience and heart, and I dare bear my testimony to it. There hath  5
not been such a service to England since the Christian religion was professed in England! I dare be bold to say it . . . We knew not and know not better how to keep the ministry good, and to augment it to goodness, than by putting such men to be Triers. Men of known integrity and piety, orthodox men and faithful. We know not how better to answer our duty to God and the Nation and the People of God, in  10
that respect, than in doing what we did.

**Cromwell to the representatives of the second Protectorate Parliament, 21 April 1657, in Carlyle vol. III**

This section concludes with two contemporary assessments of the clergy and their work during the 1650s [**3.18–3.19**]. First, here is the Presbyterian minister Richard Baxter on the 'triers':

### 3.18

Because this assembly of Triers is most heavily accused and reproached by some men, I shall speak the truth of them . . . The truth is . . . to give them their due, they did abundance of good to the Church. They saved many a congregation from ignorant, ungodly, drunken teachers . . . So that, though they were many of them somewhat partial for the Independents,[1] Separatists,[2] Fifth Monarchy men[3] and  5
Anabaptists,[4] and against the Prelatists[5] and Arminians,[6] yet so great was the benefit above the hurt which they brought to the Church, that many thousands of souls blessed God for the faithful ministers whom they let in, and grieved when the Prelatists afterwards cast them out again.

[1] 'Independents': see **3.12, note 1**.
[2] 'Separatists' = those who sought to establish their own church or sect outside the national Church.
[3] 'Fifth Monarchy men' = a religious sect which believed in the imminent rule of Christ and his saints.
[4] 'Anabaptists': see **3.12, note 2**.
[5] 'Prelatists' = hostile term for someone who supported bishops.
[6] 'Arminians' = anti-Calvinists who granted individuals a role in attaining or forfeiting salvation.

*Reliquiae Baxterianae*, **ed. M. Sylvester, book I (London, 1696)**

A rather different perspective is offered by the moderate Presbyterian Adam Martindale, who was minister in the Cheshire parish of Rotherston during the 1650s:

**3.19**

In the year 1656, the ministers of our classis[1] and many others of our neighbours agreed upon some propositions about the work of personal instruction (as many in other counties did). Multitudes of little catechisms[2] we caused to be printed, designing one for every family in our parishes, and to all, or most, they were accordingly sent. But when we actually set upon the work, even such as had     5
comparatively small parishes . . . to deal with met with great discouragements, through the unwillingness of people (especially the old ignoramusses) to have their extreme defects in knowledge searched out, the backwardness of the profane to have the smart [ = stinging] plaster of admonition applied (though lovingly) to their sores, and the business (real or pretended) left as an excuse why the persons concerned were     10
gone abroad [ = away] at the time appointed for their instruction. Beside these, the minister of Great Budworth and I had such vast parishes to go through, that multitudes of the people would be dead, in all probability, ere we could go once over them.

[1] 'classis' = group of parishes within a Presbyterian Church.
[2] 'catechisms' = elementary books for teaching Christianity, in the form of questions and answers.

*The Life of Adam Martindale, Written by Himself*, ed. R. Parkinson (Chetham Society, first series, vol. IV, 1845)

## Questions

1   Explain and comment on the following phrases:
    (i) 'weak, scandalous, popish and ill-affected persons' [3.15, lines 3–4]
    (ii) 'Whitsun-ales, wakes, morris dances, maypoles, stage plays' [3.16, lines 8–9].

2   Use **3.15** and **3.16** to summarise the objectives of the 'triers' and 'ejectors'. How realistic do you think these were?

3   Comment on the *tone* of **3.17**.

4   In what ways does **3.19** undermine the claims made in **3.17** and **3.18**?

5   What evidence *for* and *against* the arguments presented by Cromwell, Baxter and Martindale in **3.17–3.19** have you encountered elsewhere in this book, and in your wider reading?

We have seen throughout this chapter that Cromwell referred very frequently to religious issues both in public and in private. His belief in 'providences' enabled him to justify sudden changes in policy while remaining true to his long-term vision of a godly commonwealth. Yet there were those who doubted

Cromwell's sincerity. Many of his contemporaries came to believe that he was driven by ambition and self-interest, and that his references to 'providence' and 'necessity' were simply masks for policies calculated to enhance his own power. This chapter concludes with a sequence of extracts written by those who saw Cromwell as a self-seeking hypocrite. The authors came from very varied backgrounds. Document **3.20** is taken from a Leveller tract, written by a political radical who felt that his cause had been betrayed by Cromwell. Document **3.21** is a letter from a Cheshire gentleman and religious radical who did not wish to accept public office under the Protectorate. **3.22** is taken from a detailed 'Relation of England' written in 1656 by the Venetian ambassador, Giovanni Sagredo, and sent home to the Doge and Senate of Venice. Finally, **3.23** comes (like **3.18**) from the memoirs of Richard Baxter, a Presbyterian minister committed to the ideal of a broad-based national Church.

#### 3.20

You shall scarce speak to Cromwell about any thing, but he will lay his hand on his breast, elevate his eyes, and call God to record, he will weep, howl and repent, even while he doth smite you under the first rib. Captain Joyce[1] . . . can tell you sufficient stories to that purpose.

[1] 'Captain Joyce': as a Cornet (the most junior rank of commissioned officer), George Joyce (b. 1618) had arrested Charles I at Holmby House on 3 June 1647. This decisively changed the course of political events by giving the army control over the King's person. Three days earlier Cromwell had met Joyce secretly in London. Yet Cromwell denied all responsibility for the King's arrest and insisted that Joyce had acted on his own initiative. This caused a bitter quarrel between them, which formed the background to **3.20**.

**Robert Ward** *et al.*, *The Hunting of the Foxes* (London, 1649)

#### 3.21

I desire to imitate Caleb and Joshua[1] in the wilderness, as near as may be, and not to seek a confederacy with those who limit God to their passions, and against whom God hath an evident controversy etc. I believe firmly that the root and tree of piety is alive in your lordship, though the leaves thereof, through abundance of temptations and flatteries, seem to me to be withered much of late.

[1] 'Caleb and Joshua' = the two Israelites sent to spy out the land of Canaan, and who reported that it was suitable for conquest. They advised faith in God and an immediate attack, but were overruled by the majority.

**Robert Duckenfield to Cromwell, 23 March 1655, in** *A Collection of the State Papers of John Thurloe*, ed. T. Birch, vol. III (London, 1742)

**3.22**

At this point I must speak of his religion. While in general he displays a most
exemplary exterior, yet it cannot be known what rite he follows. In the late troubles
he professed himself an Anabaptist.[1] This cult denies sovereignty and claims
obedience to God alone, and to these Independents[2] belonged the majority of the
Parliament which passed sentence on the King. The moment Cromwell was          5
elevated to power, he not only broke off from the Independents, but condemned
and persecuted them. Thus he has changed his creed in accordance with interests of
state, and he thinks it suits his policy that 246 religions should be professed in
London, all alike in hostility to the Pope, but differing greatly from each other and
incompatible. This division into so many sects makes them all weak, so that no one     10
is strong enough to cause him apprehension.

[1] 'Anabaptist': see 3.12, note 2.
[2] 'Independents': see 3.12, note 1.

'Relation of England' by Giovanni Sagredo, Venetian ambassador in
England, 1656, in *Calendar of State Papers Venetian*, ed. A.B. Hinds,
vol. XXX (1655–6)

**3.23**

If after so many others I may speak my opinion of Cromwell, I think that, having
been a prodigal in his youth, and afterwards changed to a zealous religiousness, he
meant honestly in the main course of his life till prosperity and success corrupted
him . . . Hereupon Cromwell's general religious zeal giveth way to the power of that
ambition which still increaseth as his successes do increase: both piety and ambition     5
concurred in his countenancing of all that he thought godly: and charity as men; and
ambition secretly telleth him what use he might make of them. He meaneth well in
all this at the beginning, and thinketh he doth all for the safety of the godly and the
public good, but not without an eye for himself.

*Reliquiae Baxterianae*, ed. M. Sylvester, book I (London, 1696)

## Questions

1   When Captain Joyce (then a Cornet) [3.20, lines 3–4] seized the King at
    Holmby House on 3 June 1647, Cromwell expressed total surprise. Three
    days before, he had had a long talk with Joyce, in his garden and out of
    earshot. How does 3.20 help us to explain this episode?
2   What might Robert Duckenfield have had in mind when he wrote that the
    leaves of Cromwell's piety were 'withered much of late' [3.21, line 5]?
3   How far do documents 3.20–3.23 express similar criticisms of Cromwell,
    and how far do they conflict?

4  What evidence *for* and *against* the statement that Cromwell 'changed his creed in accordance with interests of state' [**3.22, lines 7–8**] have you encountered in this chapter (and elsewhere)?

5  What evidence *for* and *against* Richard Baxter's verdict [**3.23**] have you encountered in this chapter (and elsewhere)?

6  Discuss and debate the following two descriptions of Cromwell:
  (i) 'a canting hypocrite'
  (ii) 'a soldier and statesman driven on by religious imperatives'.

# 4 Cromwell's social attitudes

We saw in Chapter 2 that Cromwell wielded unprecedented power during the 1650s. He had the opportunity, if he so wished, not only to change the institutions of government but also to reform the nature of English society. Yet his precise attitudes towards the social hierarchy remain highly controversial. Many historians describe Cromwell as a social conservative, a country gentleman who wished to preserve the existing structure of society and his place within it. They contrast this reactionary opposition to social change with Cromwell's religious radicalism and willingness to experiment with constitutional forms. But other historians, such as Ivan Roots (see Bibliography, p. 114), have suggested that Cromwell wished to establish 'the rule of the saints' – a society led by the godly rather than by traditional landowners. Still others, such as Christopher Hill (see Bibliography, p. 114), have argued that Cromwell did have an authentic vision of a freer, more equal and more just society. In this chapter, we will explore Cromwell's attitudes to seventeenth-century English society in detail. What changes (if any) did he try to promote? Did he ever pursue a coherent programme of social reform? What existing features of society did he wish to preserve? Were his social attitudes at all clear or consistent? And what did those who sought radical social reform (such as the Levellers) think of Cromwell?

We begin with three extracts [4.1–4.3] which reveal Cromwell's attitude towards England's social structure, and towards those who wished to overturn it. 4.1 is taken from one of Cromwell's contributions to the Army Council debates held at Putney on 28 October–1 November 1647. These 'Putney Debates' saw a series of clashes between those officers (such as Colonel Thomas Rainborowe and Lieutenant-Colonel Edward Sexby) who supported the Levellers' demands for greater social equality, and those army leaders (including Cromwell and his son-in-law Henry Ireton) who favoured a more cautious approach. The franchise was a particularly contentious issue. On 29 October, Rainborowe strongly urged that every adult male should have the vote in parliamentary elections. Cromwell's reply was as follows:

**4.1**

I know nothing but this, that they that are the most yielding have the greatest wisdom; but really, Sir, this is not as right as it should be. No man says that you have a mind to anarchy, but the consequence of this rule tends to anarchy, must end in anarchy. For where is there any bound or limit set if you take away this limit that men that have no interest but the interest of breathing shall have no voice in     5
elections.

**Cromwell to the General Council of the Army at Putney, 29 October 1647, in Carlyle vol. III**

As we shall see [4.18], this speech contributed to the growing hostility felt towards Cromwell by many Levellers. Nearly seven years later, in his opening speech to the first Protectorate Parliament [4.2], Cromwell reflected on the hierarchical nature of society, and on the challenge which radical movements such as the Levellers posed to it.

**4.2**

What was our condition? What was the face that was upon our affairs . . . as to the interest of the nation; to the magistracy; to the rank and orders of men, whereby England hath been known for hundreds of years? A nobleman, a gentleman, a yeoman; the distinction of these, that is a good interest of the nation, and a great one! The natural magistracy of the nation, was it not almost trampled under foot . . .   5
by men of Levelling principles? I beseech you, for the orders of men and ranks of men, did not that Levelling principle tend to the reducing [of] all to an equality? . . . What was the purport of it but to make the tenant as liberal a fortune as the landlord? Which, I think, if obtained would not have lasted long! The men of that principle, after they had served their own turns, would have cried up interest and   10
property then fast enough! . . . This thing did and might extend far, because it was a pleasing voice to all poor men, and truly not unwelcome to all bad men.

**Cromwell to the first Protectorate Parliament, 4 September 1654, in Carlyle vol. II**

Another perspective on these issues is provided by the Venetian secretary in England, Lorenzo Paulucci. 4.3 comes from one of his despatches, dated 18 July 1653, and explains Barebone's Parliament in terms of Cromwell's attitudes to government and society.

4.3

This Representative [ = Barebone's Parliament] has been exhorted to dispatch all matters promptly in accordance with reason and justice . . . It is to sit until 4 November 1654; it will then be considered dissolved and succeeded by a new one. From this it appears that General Cromwell intends to preserve an aristocratic form of government.

**Lorenzo Paulucci, Venetian secretary in England, to Giovanni Sagredo, Venetian ambassador in France, 18 July 1653, in** *Calendar of State Papers Venetian*, **ed. A.B. Hinds, vol. XXIX (1653–4)**

## Questions

1   What do you think Cromwell means by the following phrases:
    (i) 'a good interest of the nation' [4.2, line 4]
    (ii) 'The natural magistracy of the nation' [4.2, line 5]?
2   What do you think the Venetian secretary means by the phrase 'an aristocratic form of government' [4.3, lines 4–5]?
3   Summarise Cromwell's attitude to the parliamentary franchise [4.1].
4   What is Cromwell's attitude to the existing structure of society, and how does he justify it [4.2]? How persuasive do you find his arguments?
5   What is Cromwell's attitude to the Levellers, and how does he justify it [4.1–4.2]? How persuasive do you find his arguments?
6   What do you think were Cromwell's motives for holding these views, and for expressing them on these occasions?
7   Do 4.1 and 4.2 provide evidence for the opinion expressed in 4.3? In what ways?

Even if Cromwell wished to preserve the existing *structure* of society, it does not necessarily follow that he was also satisfied with contemporary social *values*. The next three documents [4.4–4.6] indicate the changes which Cromwell sought to achieve in people's attitudes, in their hearts and minds. 4.4 is drawn from Cromwell's letter to William Lenthall, Speaker of the House of Commons, written the day after his victory over the Scots at Dunbar (3 September 1650). It argues that a programme of social reform should follow this decisive military success. 4.5 and 4.6 are both taken from Cromwell's opening speech to the second Protectorate Parliament on 17 September 1656. Document 4.5 discusses the need for a 'reformation of manners', while 4.6 defends the Major-Generals' enforcement of this 'reformation'.

### 4.4

It is easy to say, the Lord has done this.[1] It would do you good to see and hear our poor foot going up and down making their boast of God. But, Sir, it is in your hands, and by these eminent mercies God puts it more into your hands, to give glory to Him; to improve your power, and His blessings, to His praise. We that serve you beg of you not to own us, but God alone; we pray you own His people      5
more and more, for they are the chariots and horsemen of Israel. Disown yourselves, but own your authority, and improve it to curb the proud and insolent, such as would disturb the tranquillity of England, though under what specious pretences soever; relieve the oppressed, hear the groans of poor prisoners in England; be pleased to reform the abuses of all professions; and if there be any one      10
that makes many poor to make a few rich, that suits not a Commonwealth.

[1] 'this' = Cromwell's victory over the Scots at the battle of Dunbar, 3 September 1650.

**Cromwell to William Lenthall, Speaker of the House of Commons,
4 September 1650, in Carlyle vol. II**

### 4.5

Truly, there might be some other things offered to you in point of reformation: a reformation of manners . . . In my conscience, it was a shame to be a Christian within these fifteen, sixteen or seventeen years in this nation! Whether in Caesar's house or elsewhere! It was a shame, it was a reproach to a man; and the badge of 'Puritan' was put upon it. We would keep up nobility and gentry: and the way to      5
keep them up is not to suffer them to be patronisers and countenancers of debauchery and disorders! And you will hereby be as labourers in that work of keeping them up . . . It is a thing I am confident our liberty and prosperity depend upon – reformation. Make it a shame to see men bold in sin and profaneness, and God will bless you. You will be a blessing to the nation, and by this will be more      10
repairers of breeches than by anything in the world. Truly these things do respect the souls of men, and the spirits, which *are* the men. The mind is the man. If that be kept pure, a man signifies somewhat; if not, I would very fain see what difference there is betwixt him and a beast.

**Cromwell to the second Protectorate Parliament, 17 September 1656, in Carlyle vol. II**

### 4.6

When this insurrection [ = Penruddock's Rising] was . . . there was a little thing invented, which was the erecting of your Major-Generals, to have a little inspection upon the people thus divided, thus discontented, thus dissatisfied, split into divers interests by the workings of the popish party! . . . Truly, I think if ever anything were justifiable as to necessity, and honest in every respect, this was . . . I hope they      5

[ = the Major-Generals] are men . . . of known integrity and fidelity, and men that
have freely adventured their blood and lives for that good cause . . . And truly
England doth yet receive one day more of lengthening out its tranquillity, by that
same service of theirs . . . It hath been effectual for the preservation of your peace.
It hath been more effectual towards the discountenancing of vice and settling          10
religion than anything done these fifty years. I will abide by it, notwithstanding the
envy and slander of foolish men.

**Cromwell to the second Protectorate Parliament, 17 September 1656, in
Carlyle vol. II**

## Questions

1    Explain and comment on the following phrases:
    (i) 'the chariots and horsemen of Israel' [**4.4, line 6**]
    (ii) 'a reformation of manners' [**4.5, lines 1–2**]
    (iii) 'Whether in Caesar's house or elsewhere' [**4.5, lines 3–4**].
2    How convincing do you find Cromwell's justification of the Major-
    Generals in **4.6**? Explain your answer.
3    Using **4.4–4.6**, summarise what changes Cromwell wished to see in society,
    and why.
4    Are these changes compatible with the views which Cromwell expressed in
    **4.1** and **4.2**? Justify your response.

But did Cromwell want more than a 'reformation of manners'? Were his social
policies more dynamic, more radical, more far-reaching than that? The
following group of documents [**4.7–4.9**] looks at how far Cromwell's religious
beliefs influenced his social attitudes. The extracts throw light on whether
Cromwell wanted to establish the godly as leaders of society, to create 'the rule
of the saints'.

    In September 1643, Cromwell wrote to Sir William Springe and Mr
Maurice Barrowe, two leading members of the Suffolk County Committee,
offering advice on how to recruit soldiers to fight for Parliament:

### 4.7

I beseech you be careful what captains of horse you choose, what men be mounted:
a few honest men are better than numbers . . . If you choose godly, honest men to
be captains of horse, honest men will follow them . . . I had rather have a plain

russet-coated[1] captain that knows what he fights for, and loves what he knows, than that which you call a gentleman and is nothing else. I honour a gentleman that is so  5 indeed.

[1] 'russet-coated' = wearing a coat of reddish-brown cloth, which often denoted a humble background.

**Cromwell to Sir William Springe and Mr Maurice Barrowe, [?] September 1643, in Carlyle vol. I**

This approach was not confined to military matters. The preamble to the summons sent to each member of Barebone's Parliament on 6 June 1653 declared:

### 4.8

Forasmuch as upon the dissolution of the late Parliament [ = the Rump Parliament] it became necessary that the peace, safety and good government of this Commonwealth should be provided for; and, in order thereunto, divers persons fearing God, and of approved fidelity and honesty, are by myself, with the advice of my council of officers, nominated, to whom the great charge and trust of so weighty  5 affairs is to be committed; and having good assurance of your love to, and courage for, God and the interest of His cause, and of the good people of this Commonwealth . . .

**Summons to a member of Barebone's Parliament, 6 June 1653, in** *The Constitutional Documents of the Puritan Revolution, 1625–1660,* **ed. S.R. Gardiner (Oxford, 1899)**

When Barebone's Parliament met on 4 July 1653, Cromwell outlined the principles which guided his promotions in both the army and the commonwealth:

### 4.9

If I were to choose any servant, the meanest officer of the army or the commonwealth, I would choose a godly man that hath principles. Especially where a trust is to be committed. Because I know where to have a man that hath principles. I believe if any one of you should choose a servant, you would do thus. And I would all our magistrates were so chosen: this may be done; there may be good effects of  5 this! Surely it's our duty to choose men that fear the Lord, and will praise the Lord: such hath the Lord formed for Himself; and He expects no praises from other than such.

**Cromwell to Barebone's Parliament, 4 July 1653, in Carlyle vol. II**

## Questions

1   Explain and comment on the phrase 'the good people of this Common-wealth' [4.8, lines 7–8].
2   How far do 4.7 and 4.8 suggest that Cromwell practised what he preached in 4.9?
3   How far do 4.8 and 4.9 bear out the Venetian secretary's assessment of the significance of Barebone's Parliament [4.3]?
4   From the evidence in 4.7–4.9, would you say that Cromwell wished to establish 'the rule of the saints'? What justification do you have for your answer?
5   Are the social attitudes expressed in 4.7–4.9 compatible or incompatible with those which you have encountered earlier in this chapter?

There was, however, another side to Cromwell's social attitudes. At times, his aims seemed quite modest and limited. After all, he ruled England immediately after the shattering experience of the Civil Wars, and some of his speeches called simply for a return to peace, for 'healing and settling'. The next three documents [4.10–4.12] all develop this theme. 4.10 is taken from Cromwell's opening address to Barebone's Parliament, and advocates 'healing and looking forward'. 4.11, an extract from Cromwell's speech to the first Protectorate Parliament, makes an impassioned call for 'healing and settling'. 4.12 comes from Cromwell's closing speech to the same Parliament, and castigates it for failing to achieve this ideal.

### 4.10

I think I may say for myself and my fellow officers that we have rather desired and studied healing and looking-forward than to rake into sores and to look backward – to give things forth in those colours that would not be very pleasing to any good eye to look upon . . . It hath been full in our hearts and thoughts to desire and use all the fair and lawful means we could to have had the nation reap the fruit of all the       5
blood and treasure that had been spent in this cause: and we have had many desires and thirstings in our spirits to find out ways and means wherein we might be anywise instrumental to help it forward.

**Cromwell to Barebone's Parliament, 4 July 1653, in Carlyle vol. II**

**4.11**

That which I judge to be the end of your meeting, the great end . . . [is] healing and
settling. And the remembering of transactions too particularly, perhaps instead of
healing, at least in the hearts of many of you, may set the wound fresh a-bleeding.
And I must profess this unto you, whatever thoughts pass upon me, that if this day,
that is this meeting, prove not healing, what shall we do? But, as I said before, I        5
trust it is in the minds of you all, and much more in the mind of God, to cause
healing. It must be first in His mind, and He being pleased to put it into yours, it
will be a day indeed, and such a day as generations to come will bless you for!

**Cromwell to the first Protectorate Parliament, 4 September 1654, in Carlyle
vol. II**

**4.12**

There will be some trees that will not grow under the shadow of other trees . . . I
will tell you what hath thriven . . . under your shadow . . . Instead of peace and
settlement, instead of mercy and truth being brought together, righteousness and
peace kissing each other, by reconciling the honest people of these nations, and
settling the woeful distempers that are amongst us – which had been glorious things  5
and worthy of Christians to have proposed – weeds and nettles, briars and thorns
have thriven under your shadow! Dissettlement and division, discontent and
dissatisfaction, together with real dangers to the whole, have been more multiplied
within these five months of your sitting than in some years before! . . . Let not these
words seem too sharp, for they are as true as any mathematical demonstrations are,   10
or can be. I say, the enemies of the peace of these nations abroad and at home, the
discontented humours throughout these nations, which I think no man will grudge
to call by that name, or to make to allude to briers and thorns, they have nourished
themselves under your shadow!

**Cromwell to the first Protectorate Parliament, 22 January 1655, in Carlyle
vol. II**

## Questions
1   What do you think Cromwell is referring to in the following phrases:
    (i) 'the woeful distempers that are amongst us' [**4.12, line 5**]
    (ii) 'real dangers to the whole' [**4.12, line 8**]?
2   How convincing do you find Cromwell's claims in **4.10** on behalf of himself
    and his 'fellow officers'? Explain your answer.
3   What evidence *for* and *against* Cromwell's allegations against the first
    Protectorate Parliament [**4.12**] have you found in this chapter, and
    elsewhere?

4   Does **4.12** provide evidence that Cromwell's aims in **4.10** and **4.11** were unrealistic? How?

5   Are the attitudes which Cromwell expressed in **4.10–4.12** compatible or incompatible with those which you encountered earlier in this chapter? Explain your answer.


The next section [**4.13–4.16**] focuses on Cromwell's attitudes towards the law. In his opening speech to the first Protectorate Parliament [**4.13**], Cromwell laid down a detailed agenda for legal reform. He developed this theme two years later in his opening speech to the second Protectorate Parliament [**4.14**]. The following year, he claimed that much of this had been achieved [**4.15**]. However, Cromwell's speech of 17 September 1656 [**4.16**] indicated that in a national emergency he was prepared to flout the rule of law. As we shall see, this reckless approach to the laws was sharply criticised by some of Cromwell's contemporaries.


### 4.13

The government . . . hath desired to reform the laws . . . And for that end it hath called together persons, without offence be it spoken, of as great ability and as great interest as are in these nations, to consider how the laws might be made plain and short, and less chargeable to the people; how to lessen expense, for the good of the nation. And those things are in preparation, and bills prepared, which in due time    5
. . . will be tendered to you. In the meantime there hath been care taken to put the administration of the laws into the hands of just men, men of the most known integrity and ability. The Chancery[1] hath been reformed, I hope to the satisfaction of all good men: and as for the things, or causes, depending there, which made the burden and work of honourable persons intrusted in those services too heavy for    10
their ability, it [ = the government] hath referred many of them to those places where Englishmen love to have their rights tried, the Courts of Law at Westminster.

[1] 'Chancery' = a court of equity, and the highest court of law after the House of Lords.

**Cromwell to the first Protectorate Parliament, 4 September 1654, in Carlyle vol. II**


### 4.14

There is one general grievance in the nation. It is the law. Not that the laws are a grievance, but there are laws that are a grievance, and the great grievance lies in the execution and administration. I think I may say it, I have as eminent judges in this land as have been had, or that the nation has had, for these many years. Truly I

could be particular as to the executive part of it, to administration of the law, but     5
that would trouble you. But the truth of it is, there are wicked and abominable laws
that it will be in your power to alter. To hang a man for six pence, thirteen pence, I
know not what; to hang for a trifle, and pardon murder, is in the ministration of the
law, through the ill-framing of it. I have known in my experience abominable
murders acquitted. And to come and see men lose their lives for petty matters, this     10
is a thing God will reckon for. And I wish it may not lie upon this nation a day
longer than you have an opportunity to give a remedy; and I hope I shall cheerfully
join with you in it. This hath been a great grief to many honest hearts and
conscientious people, and I hope it is all in your hearts to rectify it.

**Cromwell to the second Protectorate Parliament, 17 September 1656, in
Carlyle vol. II**

### 4.15

I think I may say it . . . though I would be loath to say anything vainly, but since
the beginning of that change [ = the Protectorate] unto this day, I do not think there
hath been a freer procedure of the laws, not even in those years called, and not
unworthily, the 'halcyon days of peace', in Queen Elizabeth's and King James's and
King Charles's time. I do not think but that the laws proceed with as much freedom     5
and justice, and with less private solicitation as they did in those years . . . I do not
think . . . that the laws have had a more free exercise, more uninterrupted by any
hand of power, in those years than now; or that the judges have been less solicited
by letters or private interpositions either of my own or other men's, in double so
many years, in all those times named of peace! And if more of my lords the judges     10
were here than now are, they could tell us perhaps somewhat farther.

**Cromwell to the representatives of the second Protectorate Parliament,
13 April 1657, in Carlyle vol. III**

### 4.16

These Major-Generals have been to your peace and for your preservation . . .
which, we say, was necessity! . . . If you would make laws against the things that
God may please to dispose, laws to meet with everything that may happen, you
make a law in the face of God, and you tell God you will meet with all His
dispensations, and you will stay things whether He will or no! But if you make laws     5
of good government, that men may know how to obey and do for government, you
may make laws that have frailty and weakness; ay, and yet good laws to be observed.
But if nothing should ever be done but what is according to law, the throat of the
nation may be cut while we send for some to make a law! . . . It is a pitiful, beastly
notion to think that . . . if a government in extraordinary circumstances go beyond     10
the law even for self-preservation, it is yet to be clamoured at.

**Cromwell to the second Protectorate Parliament, 17 September 1656, in
Carlyle vol. II**

## Questions

1   Explain and comment on the following phrases:
    (i)   'men of the most known integrity and ability' [4.13, lines 7–8]
    (ii)  'the great grievance lies in the execution and administration' [4.14, lines 2–3]
    (iii) 'the throat of the nation may be cut while we send for some to make a law!' [4.16, lines 8–9].

2   Summarise Cromwell's objectives in 4.13–4.14.

3   To what extent does 4.15 indicate that these objectives had been achieved? Explain your answer.

4   In what ways does 4.16 undermine Cromwell's claims in 4.13–4.15?

5   How can Cromwell's argument in 4.16 be defended?

6   Looking back over the documents in this chapter so far, would you say that Cromwell had a coherent social policy or not? Justify your response.

7   Cromwell 'had a vision of building a more just and a less sinful society' (John Morrill, *Oliver Cromwell and the English Revolution*). Discuss and debate.

This chapter concludes with four extracts [4.17–4.20] by critics of Cromwell's social policies. Far from seeing him as an idealist, these portray him as an unscrupulous tyrant willing to disregard laws and exploit individuals for his own ends. Such charges first appeared in the late 1640s. For example, on 2 August 1648, the second-in-command of Cromwell's regiment, Major Robert Huntington, explained to the House of Commons why he wished to resign his commission. His speech was later printed [4.17]. It contained a bitter personal attack on Cromwell, who, Huntington claimed, was guided by four 'principles'.

### 4.17

1   that every single man is judge of just and right, as to the good and ill of a kingdom.

2   that the interest of honest men is the interest of the kingdom, and those only are deemed honest by him that are conformable to his judgement and practice . . .     5

3   that it is lawful to pass through any form of government for the accomplishing of his ends and therefore either to purge the Houses, and to support the remaining party by force everlastingly; or to put a period to them by force, is very lawful, and suitable to the interest of honest men.

4   that it is lawful to play the knave with the knave.

**Robert Huntington, *Sundry Reasons Inducing Major Robert Huntington to Lay Down his Commission, Humbly Presented to the Honourable Houses of Parliament* [2 August 1648] (London, 1648)**

The Levellers, those radical campaigners for greater social and political equality, also became very disillusioned with Cromwell. One of the most prominent was John Lilburne, whom Cromwell had tried to help in November 1640 [1.2]. However, Lilburne regarded the conservatism which Cromwell expressed at the Putney Debates [4.1] as a betrayal. He resented even more deeply Cromwell's seizure of political power after the regicide. In *England's New Chains Discovered*, published in March 1649, Lilburne blamed Cromwell for the fact that Charles I's removal did not produce a new era of freedom and justice. Two months later, Cromwell faced a mutiny of troops at Burford, inspired by Leveller ideas. He ruthlessly suppressed this and ordered three of the ringleaders to be shot. Lilburne retaliated with *An Impeachment of High Treason against Oliver Cromwell* [4.18], which appeared on 10 August 1649.

### 4.18

I must . . . talk of Lieutenant-General Cromwell, and his late gross apostasy from patronising the people's liberties and freedoms . . . It was declared with admiration and astonishment that Lieutenant-General Cromwell, who was once the glory of Englishmen in visibly appearing for justice and freedom, both against the King, the Earl of Manchester and the whole House of Peers, etc., and who had a principal    5
hand in so many gallant declarations of the army in which freedom, righteousness and justice was published to the whole kingdom most gloriously, that this very Lieutenant-General Cromwell (whose name for honesty once rung and echoed throughout England) should now apostate from his former declared gallantry and honesty and turn his back upon his own solemn declarations, remonstrances and    10
engagements, and persecute with bitterness (even to death and bonds) righteousness, truth and justice, in all those in the army he met with it in (and now of late became a grand patron, protector and earnest pleader for the preservation of all the grand corrupt and enslaving interests in England) was a wonder and astonishment, that he had the gloriest [ = most glorious] praise and opportunity put    15
into his hands that ever God put into the hands of an Englishman, to do good unto his native country, and to settle the laws, liberties and peace thereof in their lustre and glory, should be courted out of all his principles, protestations and engagements by a little selfish, glittering, worldly or corrupt honour, and to convert his power and interest to the quite contrary, to make us slaves and vassals, was the admiration    20
and wonder of all knowing, observing and unbiased Englishmen, and the greatest mischief that ever befel the honest men of the kingdom.

**John Lilburne,** *An Impeachment of High Treason against Oliver Cromwell* (London, 1649)

Lilburne was tried for treason in October 1649 and spent the rest of the Interregnum in prison. Yet, although the Levellers were a spent force after

1649, criticism continued to dog Cromwell until his death. One of the most frequent targets was his alleged willingness to by-pass the laws and to rule according to his own will. In this respect he was sometimes compared unfavourably with Charles I. A good example is the anonymous *The Picture of a New Courtier Drawn in a Conference between Mr Timeserver and Mr Plainheart* [4.19], published in 1656.

#### 4.19

'Plain[heart]: . . . The difference that is lyeth only in this, that his [ = Cromwell's] little finger is thicker than the King's loins, as will appear by these considerations. First, his imprisoning of men contrary to law, at his own will and pleasure; yea, many of the Commonwealth's best friends, and have kept them in prison many months together without seeing the face of any accuser or coming to any trial at law,    5 the truth of which may be evinced by many instances, viz. . . . [then follows a list of fifteen names, including Major-General Thomas Harrison,[1] Edmund Ludlow[2] and John Lilburne[3]] . . . that are forced to drink of the same cup of his will and pleasure: so that we may say, the King chastised us with whips, but Cromwell chastises us with scorpions.

[1] 'Thomas Harrison' = Fifth Monarchist and leading advocate of Barebone's Parliament.
[2] 'Edmund Ludlow' = a former Parliamentarian general and member of the Long Parliament who turned against Cromwell after the dissolution of the Rump (see **2.19** and **5.25**).
[3] 'John Lilburne': see **4.18**.

*The Picture of a New Courtier Drawn in a Conference between Mr Timeserver and Mr Plainheart* (London, 1656)

The same charge of lawlessness was developed after Cromwell's death in Slingsby Bethel's *The World's Mistake in Oliver Cromwell* [4.20]. (For other extracts from this work, see **2.17** and **5.26**.)

#### 4.20

To prove the . . . assertion that Oliver's time was full of oppression and injustice, I shall but instance . . . a few particulars, and begin with John Lilburne[1] . . . for, contrary to law, [Cromwell] kept him in prison, until he was so far spent in consumption [ = tuberculosis] that he only turned out to die. [Second]ly, Mr Cony's[2] is so notorious that it needs little more than naming. He was a prisoner at    5 Cromwell's suit, and being brought to the King's Bench bar by a *habeas corpus*, had his counsel taken from the bar, and sent to the Tower for no other reason than the pleading of their client's cause; an act of violence that I believe the whole story of

England does not parallel. [Third]ly, . . . [Cromwell] invited all God's people in his Declaration[3] to offer him their advice in the weighty matters then upon his shoulders. Sir Henry [Vane][4] taking a rise from hence offered his advice by a treatise called *The Healing Question*.[5] But Cromwell, angry at being taken at his word, seized, imprisoned and endeavoured to proceed further against him, for doing only what he had invited him to do; and some may think that Sir Henry suffered justly, for having known [Cromwell] so long, and yet . . . trust anything he said . . . [Fifth]ly . . . that Cromwell, who was the principal person in procuring that law,[6] when he thought it for his advantage not to keep it, was the only man for breaking it.

10

15

[1] 'John Lilburne': see **4.18**.
[2] 'Mr Cony' = George Cony, a London merchant, who in 1655 refused to pay customs duties not imposed by Act of Parliament.
[3] 'his Declaration' = *A Declaration of his Highness [the Lord Protector], Inviting the People of England and Wales to a Day of Solemn Fasting and Humiliation* (London, [March] 1656).
[4] 'Sir Henry Vane' = an Independent, republican and member of the Council of State, imprisoned in September 1656.
[5] '*The Healing Question*' = Sir Henry Vane, *A Healing Question Propounded and Resolved* (London, [August] 1656).
[6] 'that law' = the Decimation Tax of May 1655, whereby all Royalists and other disaffected persons had to pay an income tax of 10 per cent.

**Slingsby Bethel,** *The World's Mistake in Oliver Cromwell* **(London, 1668)**

## Questions

1   Explain and comment on the following phrases:
   (i) 'the interest of honest men is the interest of the kingdom' [**4.17, line 3**]
   (ii) 'the greatest mischief that ever befel the honest men of the kingdom' [**4.18, lines 21–2**]
   (iii) 'the King chastised us with whips, but Cromwell chastises us with scorpions' [**4.19, lines 9–10**].

2   How far are **4.17–4.20** expressing similar or different criticisms of Cromwell?

3   From the evidence you have seen in this chapter, and elsewhere, would you say that the charges in each of **4.17–4.20** were *justified*?

4   'The various printed attacks on Cromwell tell us as much about their authors as they do about Cromwell.' Discuss and debate.

5   Comment on the following two assessments of Cromwell:
   (i) 'a champion of social reform and civil liberties'
   (ii) 'an opponent of social change who disregarded popular democratic rights'.

# 5 Cromwell and the world

In this chapter we turn away from Cromwell's handling of domestic affairs to examine his policies towards the rest of Britain and the world. What were his objectives on the international scene? Were they at all consistent? How did they fit in with the attitudes to domestic issues which we have already explored? And did Cromwell have any lasting impact on England's position within the British Isles and in the wider world?

We begin with Cromwell's 'British policy'. In the seventeenth century, English monarchs were also kings of Scotland and Ireland, and princes of Wales, and an ability to manage this 'multiple monarchy' was essential for political survival. Developments in the three kingdoms and the principality of Wales were often closely connected. Most spectacularly, rebellions in Scotland (1638–40) and Ireland (1641) helped to precipitate the outbreak of the English Civil Wars in 1642. Recently, a number of historians, led by John Morrill, Conrad Russell and David Stevenson, have suggested that we should label the events of the 1640s 'the crisis of the three kingdoms', or 'the general crisis of the British Isles'. The origins, course and outcome of the English Civil Wars can only be understood within a British context. It is also fruitful to apply this British perspective to the 1650s. In 1649–51, Cromwell, victor of the English Civil Wars, faced an urgent need to conquer and settle both Scotland and Ireland. The first part of this chapter deals in turn with Cromwell's attitudes towards these two kingdoms; with his attempts to bring them under English control; and with the resistance which he encountered.

During the Civil Wars, the Scots had twice sent armies into England, to assist first Parliament (1644–5), then the King (1648). We have already examined Cromwell's attitude towards the second invasion [1.21]. In August 1648 he defeated the Scots at Preston [1.20], and then marched north of the border. However, he appears to have treated the Scots fairly leniently. In a letter written to his cousin Robert Hammond on 6 November 1648 [5.1] he explained his motives.

**5.1**

I have prayed . . . for the day to see union and right understanding between the
godly people (Scots, English, Jews, Gentiles, Presbyterians,[1] Independents,[2]
Anabaptists[3] and all). Our brothers of Scotland (really Presbyterians) were our
greatest enemies. God hath justified us in their sight, caused us to requite good for
evil, caused them to acknowledge it publicly by acts of state, and privately, and the     5
thing is true in the light of the sun . . . Was it not fit to be civil, to profess love, to
deal with clearness with them for removing of prejudice, to ask them what they had
against us, and to give them an honest answer? This we have done, and not more.
And herein is a more glorious work in our eyes than if we had gotten the sacking
and plunder of Edinburgh, the strong castles into our hands, and made conquest     10
from Tweed to the Orcades [ = the Orkney Islands]; and we can say, through God
we have left by the grace of God such a witness amongst them, as if it work not yet
there is that conviction upon them that will undoubtedly bear its fruit in due time.

[1] 'Presbyterians' = advocates or members of a national Church organised around local,
provincial and national assemblies.
[2] 'Independents' = those opposed to a national Church, who believe that each congregation
should be independent.
[3] 'Anabaptists' = a religious sect believing that only those baptised as adults can achieve
salvation.

**Cromwell to Colonel Robert Hammond, 6 November 1648, in Carlyle
vol. III**

Yet when Charles I was beheaded the Scots immediately proclaimed his son
Charles II as their king, and as king of England and Ireland too. England faced
the threat of an imminent Royalist invasion. In 1649–51 Cromwell therefore
launched a series of campaigns to remove this danger. He first conquered
Ireland (see **3.5** and **5.6**) and then turned against the Scots, defeating them at
the battles of Dunbar (3 September 1650) and Worcester (3 September 1651).
These decisive victories left the problem of how to govern Scotland. A
declaration [**5.2**], drawn up in October 1651 and published in February 1652,
indicated Cromwell's main aims.

**5.2**

The Parliament of the Commonwealth of England . . . declare[s]: 1. . . . that their
constant endeavours shall be to promote the preaching of the gospel [in Scotland],
and to advance the power of true religion and holiness, and that God may be served
and worshipped . . . with protection, and all due countenance and encouragement
therein to the people of that nation, from those in authority under the Parliament.     5
2. . . . Scotland shall . . . be incorporated into, and become one Commonwealth with
this of England . . . 3. . . . all the estates whatsoever, real or personal, of those who

did invade England, under [the] Duke [of] Hamilton in the year 1648, or were
advising, contriving, or promoting thereof, or in any way aiding, abetting or
assisting thereunto . . . shall be confiscated and forfeited to the use and benefit of          10
the Commonwealth of England . . . 4. . . . all such persons of the Scottish nation as
are not comprehended within the former qualifications, but have kept themselves
free from the guilt of those things which have compelled this war, and shall now . . .
concur with and promote the ends formerly and now declared by the Parliament,
shall be taken into the protection of the Parliament, and enjoy the liberties and          15
estates, as other . . . free people of the Commonwealth of England . . . [Those] who
put themselves under the protection of the Parliament of the Commonwealth of
England . . . shall . . . be set free from their former dependencies and bondage-
services, and shall be admitted as tenants, freeholders and heritors . . . to live . . .
like a free people delivered (through God's goodness) from their former slaveries,          20
vassalage and oppressions.

**'A Declaration of the Parliament of the Commonwealth of England,
concerning the Settlement of Scotland', 28 October 1651, in** *The
Cromwellian Union*, **ed. C.S. Terry (Scottish History Society, vol. XL, 1902)**

The response of the Scots varied from the lukewarm to the hostile. **5.3** comes
from the list of reasons why Scotland's second city, Glasgow, opposed
Cromwell's plans.

### 5.3

It doth by necessary and clear consequence establish in the Church a vast and
boundless toleration of all sorts of error and heresies without any effectual
[ = effective] remedy for suppressing the same; notwithstanding that there be the
same moral and perpetual obligation upon us to suppress and extirpate heresy no
less than profaneness; likeas [ = likewise] this declaration do allow diverse ways of          5
worshipping God under the name of gospel ways.

**'Reasons for the Dissent of Glasgow', 24 February 1652, in** *The Cromwellian
Union*, **ed. C.S. Terry (Scottish History Society, vol. XL, 1902)**

Nevertheless, the union of England and Scotland was formalised by an
ordinance [**5.4**] issued on 12 April 1654.

### 5.4

His Highness the Lord Protector of the Commonwealth of England, Scotland and
Ireland etc., taking into consideration how much it may conduce to the glory of God
and the peace and welfare of the people of this whole island, that after all these late
unhappy wars and differences, the people of Scotland should be united with the

people of England into one Commonwealth and under one Government . . .                    5
[announces that] Scotland . . . [is] hereby incorporated into, constituted,
established, declared and confirmed one Commonwealth with England; and in every
Parliament to be held successively for the said Commonwealth, thirty persons shall
. . . serve for Scotland . . . All customs, excise and other imposts for goods
transported from England to Scotland, and from Scotland to England, by sea or          10
land, . . . shall be taken off and discharged . . . All cesses [ = assessments], public
impositions and taxations whatsoever [shall] be imposed, taxed and levied from
henceforth proportionably from the whole people of this union so united.

'An Ordinance by the Protector for the Union of England and Scotland',
12 April 1654, in *The Constitutional Documents of the Puritan Revolution,
1625–1660*, ed. S.R. Gardiner (Oxford, 1899)

What, then, was the impact of the Cromwellian Union on Scotland? Contemporary opinions were very mixed. Many Scots complained of severe and
widespread poverty: as the Presbyterian minister Robert Baillie put it, 'the
English have all the money'. On the other hand, English observers could point
to benefits such as the abolition of feudal tenure and the easing of oppressive
rule by the Presbyterian Church. In his last great parliamentary speech on
25 January 1658 [5.5], Cromwell offered his own assessment of Scotland's
fortunes during the 1650s.

### 5.5

Hath Scotland been long settled? Have they not a . . . sense of poverty? I speak
plainly . . . I do think the Scots nation have been under as great a suffering, in point
of livelihood and subsistence outwardly, as any people I have yet named to you. I do
think truly they are a very ruined nation. And yet in a way (I have spoken with
some gentlemen come from thence) hopeful enough yet. It hath pleased God to give   5
that plentiful encouragement to the meaner sort . . . in Scotland . . . The meaner
sort in Scotland live as well, and are likely to come into as thriving a condition
under your government as when they were under their own great lords, who made
them work for their living no better than the peasants of France. I am loath to speak
anything that may reflect upon that nation. But the middle sort of this people grow   10
up there into such a substance as makes their lives comfortable, if not better than
they were before.

**Cromwell to the second Protectorate Parliament, 25 January 1658, in
Carlyle vol. III**

## Questions

1  Explain and comment on the following phrases:
   (i) 'to deal with clearness with them for removing of prejudice' [**5.1**, **lines 6–7**]
   (ii) 'a vast and boundless toleration of all sorts of error and heresies' [**5.3**, **lines 1–2**].

2  Using **5.1–5.2** and **5.4–5.5**, summarise Cromwell's attitude towards Scotland and the Scots.

3  From the evidence in **5.1–5.5**, and your wider reading, what were the benefits of Cromwellian rule in Scotland?

4  From the evidence in **5.1–5.5**, and your wider reading, what were the drawbacks of Cromwellian rule in Scotland?

5  How far were Cromwell's Scottish policies consistent or inconsistent with the attitudes which you have encountered earlier in this book? Explain your answer.

6  'Cromwell hoped that the English would bring to Scotland not just the sword, but godliness, liberty and prosperity' (David Stevenson, 'Cromwell, Scotland and Ireland', in *Oliver Cromwell and the English Revolution*, ed. John Morrill). Discuss and debate.

Cromwell's policies towards Scotland may be compared and contrasted with his treatment of Ireland. In October 1641, the Catholics of Ulster had rebelled and massacred over three thousand Protestants. Their claim to be acting on Charles I's orders, though false, was crucial in the breakdown of trust between the King and the English Parliament. During the first and second Civil Wars, Parliament constantly feared a Royalist-inspired invasion from Ireland. Such fears increased dramatically in the spring of 1649, when Charles II favoured Ireland as the base for an attempt to regain the English throne. On 23 March, Cromwell reviewed the situation in a speech [**5.6**] to the newly created Council of State.

### 5.6

[In Ireland] all the papists and the King's party – I cannot say all the papists, but the greater part of them – are in a very strong combination against you . . . If we do not endeavour to make good our interest there, and that timely [= in time], we shall not only have . . . our interest rooted out there, but they will in a very short time be able to land forces in England, and to put us to trouble here . . . I had [= would]    5
rather be overrun with a Cavalierish interest than a Scotch interest; I had rather be

overrun with a Scotch interest than an Irish interest; and I think of all this is the most dangerous. If they shall be able to carry on their work, they will make [us] the most miserable people in the earth, for all the world knows their barbarism.

**Cromwell to the Council of State, 23 March 1649, in Carlyle vol. III**

The Council of State therefore decided to send a military expedition, and Cromwell landed at Dublin on 15 August. His rapid conquest of Ireland included the famous massacres of Drogheda (11 September) and Wexford (11 October). We have already examined Cromwell's account of events at Wexford [3.5]. Later, on 31 December, he reflected on his campaign in a letter [5.7] to John Sadler, one of the Masters of the Court of Chancery in London.

### 5.7

A Divine Presence hath gone along with us in the late great transactions in [Ireland] . . . To us who are employed as instruments in this work the contentment that appears is that we are doing our master's [ = God's] work, that we have His presence and blessing with us . . . We find the people very greedy after the Word, and flocking to Christian meetings; much of that prejudice that lies upon poor    5 people in England being a stranger to their minds . . . Sir, it seems that we have a great opportunity to set up, until the Parliament shall otherwise determine, a way of doing justice amongst these poor people, which, for the uprightness and cheapness of it, may exceedingly gain upon them, who have been accustomed to as much injustice, tyranny and oppression from their landlords, the great men, and those that    10 should have done them right, as, I believe, any people in that which we call Christendom . . . Sir, if justice were freely and impartially administered here, the foregoing darkness and corruption would make it look so much the more glorious and beautiful, and draw more hearts after it.

**Cromwell to John Sadler, 31 December 1649, in Carlyle vol. III**

Earlier in December, however, Irish church leaders had met at Clonmacnoise and issued a declaration warning that Cromwell intended to colonise Ireland. 5.8 is taken from Cromwell's reply, published in January 1650.

### 5.8

Was the English army brought over for this purpose [ = to colonise Ireland], as you allege? . . . No, I can give you a better reason for the army's coming over than this. England hath had experience of the blessing of God in prosecuting just and righteous causes, whatever the cost and hazard be. And if ever men were engaged in a righteous cause in the world, this will be scarce a second to it. We are come to ask    5 an account of the innocent blood that hath been shed; and to endeavour to bring

them to an account (by the blessing and presence of the Almighty, in whom alone is
our hope and strength), who, by appearing in arms, seek to justify the same. We
come to break the power of a company of lawless rebels, who having cast off the
authority of England, live as enemies of human society; whose principles . . . are to    10
destroy and subjugate all men not complying with them. We come (by the assistance
of God) to hold forth and maintain the lustre and glory of English liberty in a nation
where we have an undoubted right to do it; wherein the people of Ireland . . . may
equally participate in all benefits, to use liberty and fortune equally with
Englishmen, if they keep out of arms.

'A Declaration of the Lord Lieutenant of Ireland [ = Cromwell], for the
Undeceiving of Deluded and Seduced People; which may be Satisfactory to
All that do not Wilfully Shut their Eyes against the Light . . .', January 1650,
in Carlyle vol. II

Once conquered, Ireland, like Scotland, was to be united with the English
Commonwealth. An ordinance of 12 August 1652 [**5.9**] laid down the terms of
this union.

### 5.9

Whereas the Parliament of England, after the expense of much blood and treasure
for suppression of the horrid rebellion in Ireland, have by the good hand of God
upon their undertakings brought that affair to such an issue, as that a total
reducement and settlement of that nation may, with God's blessing be speedily
effected, to the end therefore that the people of that nation may know that it is not    5
the intention of the Parliament to extirpate that whole nation, but that mercy and
pardon . . . may be extended to all . . . [who submit] themselves to the Parliament of
the Commonwealth of England and [live] peaceably and obediently under their
government . . . be it enacted and declared by this present Parliament . . . that . . .
[Then followed ten clauses excepting 'from pardon for life and estate' all Irish in    10
arms before 10 November 1642; all Catholic priests and all who helped them; and
all who had borne arms against England. All those 'of the Popish Religion' living in
Ireland at any time between 1641 and 1650 who had 'not manifested their constant
good affection to the Commonwealth of England' were to forfeit one-third of their
estates.]

'An Act for the Settling of Ireland', 12 August 1652, in *Acts and Ordinances of
the Interregnum, 1642–1660*, ed. C.H. Firth and R.S. Rait, vol. II (London,
1911)

## Questions

1. Explain and comment on the following phrases:
    (i) 'all the world knows their barbarism' [5.6, line 9]
    (ii) 'We are come to ask an account of the innocent blood that hath been shed' [5.8, lines 5–6]
    (iii) 'the horrid rebellion in Ireland' [5.9, line 2].
2. Using 5.6–5.9, summarise Cromwell's attitude towards Ireland and the Irish.
3. In what ways did the settlement of Ireland [5.9] differ from that of Scotland [5.2 and 5.4]? How do you account for the differences?
4. Did Cromwell pursue any common goals in *both* Scotland *and* Ireland? If so, what were they? Explain your answer.
5. How far would you agree with the historian who wrote that 'puritan fanaticism explains both the harsh nature of the Cromwellian Irish Settlement and the lenient nature of the Cromwellian Scottish Settlement'? Justify your response.
6. 'Cromwell had dreams of just and godly futures for Ireland and Scotland – through making them little Englands' (David Stevenson). Discuss and debate.

We now move away from Britain to explore Cromwell's wider foreign policy. He faced a very difficult situation in 1649. Most European states were horrified by the regicide and deeply suspicious of the new English republic. In Sweden and Denmark, ministers preached sermons condemning the English revolutionaries, while the Dutch government continued to address Charles II as king. France broke off trading links with England. Yet by the time Cromwell died in 1658, England had established good relations with all the major European powers except Spain, and was widely respected abroad. How did Cromwell achieve this remarkable turn-round? What objectives lay behind his foreign policy? Were they consistent with the other aims we have examined, and what methods did he use to attain them?

The remainder of this chapter is divided into five sections. First of all, there is a group of documents [5.10–5.12] examining the general principles which guided Cromwell's world policy. Then follow three case studies of Cromwell's relations with particular powers: Sweden and the Dutch [5.13–5.17]; France [5.18–5.20]; and Spain [5.21–5.24]. The final section [5.25–5.27] consists of three extracts which criticise Cromwell's foreign policy.

The motives which shaped Cromwell's foreign policy remain highly controversial. Historians are divided over how far he was guided by ideological principles or by England's economic interests. The next three documents [5.10–5.12] all throw light on this question. 5.10 is taken from a memorandum 'concerning the foreign affairs in the Protector's time' composed during the 1660s by Cromwell's Secretary of State, John Thurloe, for the guidance of Charles II and his advisers. 5.11 comes from the Swedish ambassador's account of a conversation in 1655 in which Cromwell outlined the 'fundamentals' of his foreign policy. Finally, an extract from Cromwell's speech to the second Protectorate Parliament on 25 January 1658 [5.12] indicates his view of European developments shortly before his death.

### 5.10

I find the alliances of those times were contracted and conserved upon these interests: . . . To deprive his Majesty of foreign assistance in his restitution [ = restoration]: hence it was that the alliance with France was preferred to that of Spain . . . The Cardinal[1] propounded a league offensive, to be agreed upon between England and France . . . The Protector did not much apprehend [ = recognise] the   5
usefulness of so strict a league, and therefore desired it not, yet . . . [was] willing to treat . . . [provided] 1. That France would not . . . give any assistance to the King of England . . . 2. That he might depend upon France in case of new troubles arising between him and the Dutch . . . 3. That the Protestants of France might be well treated . . . The Protector having received assurances of these things . . . a treaty   10
was concluded, only of a defensive alliance. The peace with France was followed with a war with Spain, and all future treaties and negotiations were managed with reference to that . . . Spain [was] weakened with the war with England, wherein that crown received more prejudice in three years than in ten with France; his [ = Spain's] dominions, both in Europe and America, being . . . so besieged by the   15
English fleets, that his trade into America from Spain, and his returns in silver from thence into Spain, was wholly obstructed . . . England had the opportunity . . . to be the umpire of peace between [France and Spain] . . . The Protector . . . endeavour[ed] a peace between the Dane and the Swede . . . as well to obviate the designs of the Dutch as to keep open the way of making use of the arms of Sweden   20
against the emperor . . . The Dutch had discovered [ = revealed] . . . a fixed design to monopolise all trade into their own hands . . . There were no greater considerations in England, in reference to foreign interests, than how to obviate the growing greatness of the Dutch.

[1] 'The Cardinal' = Cardinal Mazarin, the chief minister of France.

**[John Thurloe,] 'Concerning the foreign affairs in the Protector's time', in John, Baron Somers, *A Collection of Scarce and Valuable Tracts*, ed. Sir Walter Scott, vol. VI (London, 1811)**

**5.11**

[Cromwell] protest[ed] his affection to Y[our] M[ajesty] and his earnest desire for
his friendship. He then laid bare, in the greatest confidence, the *fundamenta*
[ = fundamentals] of all his policies; which were directed to no other ends than
*libertatem religionis* [ = freedom of religion] and freedom of trade. He spoke first of
Spain, and how he could have come to an understanding with them on all other          5
points if only the English in that country could have been safe from the Inquisition;
but upon this it had been impossible to reach agreement . . . As to France, the
situation had been such that neither Tunis nor Algiers[1] had done as much damage
to English merchants in the Mediterranean as they have, so that he was bound to
take strong action against them in that quarter; and he confessed that though both          10
the one and the other have for a long time as good as begged peace of him, he was
not prepared to accept it without regard to the two fundamentals to which he had
alluded. He went on to say that the Protestant powers were a mere handful in
comparison with the Catholics; and if God had not miraculously sown discord
between the Catholics themselves, he could not see how the Protestants would have          15
been able to defend themselves against them . . . As to the Dutch, he said that if
Y[our] M[ajesty] pleased he was willing to intervene with Ambassador Nieupoort[2]
to hinder their design and to resolve, in a spirit of amity, any difference that might
have arisen . . . He . . . desired . . . that God would always bless Y[our] M[ajesty] as
one of the greatest supports of the Protestant Cause.

[1] 'Tunis' and 'Algiers' = two ports on the North African coast notorious for their pirates
who attacked European shipping.
[2] 'Ambassador Nieupoort' = Willem Nieupoort, the Dutch ambassador to England.

**Christer Bonde, Swedish ambassador-extraordinary, to King Charles X of
Sweden, 28 September 1655, in *Swedish Diplomats at Cromwell's Court,
1655–6*, ed. M. Roberts (Camden Society, fourth series, vol. XXXVI, 1988)**

**5.12**

He that looks well about him, and considers the state of the Protestant affairs all
Christendom over . . . must needs say and acknowledge that the greatest design now
on foot, in comparison [with] which all other designs are but little things is, whether
the Christian world shall be all popery, or whether God has a love to, and we ought
to have a love to, and a brotherly fellow-feeling of the interest of all the Protestant          5
Christians in the world? And he that strikes at one species of a general to make it
nothing, strikes at all. Is it not so now, that the Protestant cause and interest abroad
is struck at, and is, in opinion and apprehension, quite under foot trodden down? . . .
The papacy, and those that are upholders of it, they have openly and avowedly
trodden God's people under foot, on that very notion and account, that they were          10
Protestants. The money you parted with in that noble charity that was exercised
within this nation, and the just sense that you had of those poor Piedmontese,[1] was
satisfaction enough to yourselves of that . . . But is that of Piedmont all? No. Look

but how the House of Austria, on both sides of Christendom, both in Austria and
Spain, are armed and prepared to make themselves able to destroy the whole
Protestant interest . . . [The Pope] hath influenced all the powers and all the princes
in Europe to [do] this very thing.    15

[1] 'Piedmontese': see **5.18–5.20**. Cromwell is referring here to a national collection which
raised £38,421 for the Protestants of Piedmont in 1655.

**Cromwell to the second Protectorate Parliament, 25 January 1658, in
Carlyle vol. III**


## Questions

1  Summarise the goals of Cromwell's foreign policy as outlined by John
   Thurloe in **5.10**.
2  What were the 'fundamentals' of Cromwell's foreign policy as expressed in
   **5.11**?
3  What may be gleaned from **5.12** about Cromwell's foreign policy aims in
   1658?
4  Comment on the usefulness of each of **5.10–5.12** as evidence for Cromwell's
   inner motives and beliefs.
5  How far do **5.10–5.12** reveal similar or different objectives in Cromwell's
   foreign policy? Explain your answer.
6  What can we learn from **5.10–5.12** about Cromwell's attitude towards:
   (i) the Dutch
   (ii) France
   (iii) Spain
   (iv) the cause of international Protestantism
   (v) England's economic interests?


Our first case study of Cromwell's foreign policy in action examines his
relations with the Dutch and the Swedes. By the mid-seventeenth century, the
Dutch were England's main commercial rivals. They were particularly skilled
at transporting bulky cargoes in flat-bottomed boats ('busses') at low cost. To
combat this, the Rump Parliament passed a Navigation Act on 9 October 1651
stating that all goods imported into England should be carried either in English
ships or in ships from their country of origin. The Dutch strongly objected, and
a series of skirmishes in the English Channel led to full-scale war early in July
1652. However, on 21 July Cromwell's chaplain and secretary Hugh Peter
persuaded the Dutch congregation in London to petition Parliament to resume
negotiations with the Dutch government, the States-General. The historian

Lieuwe van Aitzema, who was Hanseatic Resident at The Hague and an envoy to England in 1651–2, later recorded Cromwell's response when he saw the petition [5.13].

5.13

Lord General Cromwell declared, quoting biblical texts in his reply, that he did not like this war; that he commended this Christian exhortation; that he would do everything in his power to bring about peace. In the meantime, he would do his best.

Lieuwe van Aitzema, *Saken van Staet in Oologh, in ende omtrent de Vereeinigde Nederlanden*, vol. III (The Hague, 1669) [my translation]

The conflict nevertheless dragged on for nearly two years. But by early 1654 it was clearly turning against the Dutch: England had complete control over the Channel and had captured nearly 1,400 Dutch ships. The Dutch therefore capitulated and signed the Treaty of Westminster with England on 5 April [5.14]. The 1651 Navigation Act was to stand, and the Dutch promised to give no further assistance to Charles II. In addition, the two powers formed a defensive alliance:

5.14

I. It is agreed . . . that from this day forward there shall be a true, firm and inviolable peace, more sincere friendship, and nearer alliance, union and confederation than heretofore, betwixt the Commonwealth of England, and the States-General of the United Provinces of the Netherlands . . . V. That the two Commonwealths shall remain confederate friends, joined and allied together for the   5
defence and preservation of the liberties and freedom of the people against all whomsoever who shall attempt the disturbance of either state by sea or land.

*Articles of Peace, Union and Confederation concluded between his Highness Oliver, Lord Protector . . . and . . . the States-General of the United Provinces of the Netherlands . . . 5 April 1654* (London, 1654)

Meanwhile, in the autumn of 1653 Cromwell sent a diplomatic mission to Sweden. This was particularly appropriate during the Anglo-Dutch war: relations between the Swedes and the Dutch were often strained as they struggled for control of Baltic trade. Cromwell chose the distinguished common lawyer and administrator Bulstrode Whitelocke as ambassador to Sweden. Whitelocke later recalled Cromwell's instructions to him [5.15].

**5.15**

The business is of [as] exceeding great importance to the Commonwealth as any can be, that it is. And there is no prince or state in Christendom with whom there is any probability for us to have a friendship, but only the Queen of Sweden [= Queen Christina] . . . The business is very honourable and exceedingly likely to have good success. [The Queen's] public ministers here have already agreed upon most of the    5
material and main points of the business. If it had not been such an employment, we would not have put you upon it: the business of trade, and of the funds, and touching the Dutch, are such as there cannot be any of greater consequence . . . If you should decline it . . . the Commonwealth would suffer extremely by it . . . and the Protestant interest would suffer by it . . . No business can be of greater    10
consequence to us and our trade, wherein the Dutch will endeavour to over-reach us; and it were good to prevent them, and the Dane, and first to serve our own interest.

B. Whitelocke, *A Journal of the Swedish Embassy in the Years 1653 and 1654*, vol. I (London, 1772)

Whitelocke's embassy was successful, and the Treaty of Uppsala was signed between England and Sweden on 11 April 1654. To confirm this treaty a Swedish mission was sent to England in the spring of 1655. As we have seen [2.14; 5.11], the despatches of the Swedish envoy (Peter Julius Coyet) and the Swedish ambassador-extraordinary (Christer Bonde) contain much valuable information about Cromwell and his policies. 5.16 comes from Bonde's report of a conversation in November 1655 in which Cromwell discussed his foreign policy in general, and Dutch–Swedish relations in particular.

**5.16**

[Cromwell] then began to expound the interest the Dutch had in the trade to Prussia, and that it was not strange that they should be concerned about it. He next spoke eloquently and at length of the situation as between Catholics and Protestants . . . The theme of his speech was that the honour of God was the sole *but* [ = end] of all his actions; he recapitulated the causes of his attack on Spain, and the present    5
condition of that enterprise [see 5.21–5.24]; and he ended by saying that he would use every possible means with both sides [ = Sweden and the Dutch] to preserve amity [ = friendship] between them . . . He . . . reiterat[ed] once again how necessary it was to the Dutch that their bread-basket (which is Danzig) should be open to them, and protested his desire to remain in unity with them and serve them    10
by all practicable means; his overriding wish being to secure unity between the two

of us, for the honour of God and the interest of Protestantism, of which he spoke most earnestly, and in noble language implored me to believe in his sincerity and truth.

Christer Bonde, Swedish ambassador-extraordinary, to King Charles X of Sweden, 9 November 1655, in *Swedish Diplomats at Cromwell's Court, 1655–6*, ed. M. Roberts (Camden Society, fourth series, vol. XXXVI, 1988)

But Cromwell's hopes for a pan-Protestant league including the Dutch and the Swedes proved vain. Both powers continued to defend their trading interests in the Baltic, and relations between them remained tense. Even more annoying to England were Dutch attempts to levy dues on goods passing through the Baltic Sound. Cromwell discussed this problem in his speech to the second Protectorate Parliament on 25 January 1658 [5.17].

### 5.17

Men that are not true to the religion we profess . . . God will find them out! . . . Consider if this may seem . . . to be a design against your well-being . . . wherein so many Protestants are not so right as were to be wished! If they can shut us out of the Baltic Sea, and make themselves masters of that, where is your trade? . . . You have not yet made it your trade to prefer your profit before your godliness, but     5 reckon godliness the greater gain! But should it so happen that . . . you should not be able to vindicate yourself against all whatsoever – I mention no one state upon this head . . . judge you where you are! You have accounted yourselves happy in being environed with [ = surrounded by] a great ditch from all the world . . . You will not be able to keep your ditch, nor your shipping, unless you turn your ships     10 and shipping into troops of horse and companies of foot, and fight to defend yourselves in *terra firma* [ = on dry land]!

Cromwell to the second Protectorate Parliament, 25 January 1658, in Carlyle vol. III

## Questions

1 How convincing do you find Cromwell's promise in 5.13? Explain your answer.

2 Summarise Cromwell's reasons for seeking good relations with Sweden [5.15–5.16].

3 How far do 5.13–5.17 indicate a consistent attitude towards the Dutch? If so, what was it? If not, in what ways did it change?

4 Do 5.13–5.17 contain evidence that the principles set out in 5.10–5.12 were put into practice? Justify your response.

5   Comment on the following two assessments of Cromwell's policies towards
    the Dutch and the Swedes:
    (i) 'policies guided by religious motives and designed to serve the cause of
        international Protestantism'
    (ii) 'policies guided by economic motives and designed to serve England's
        commercial interests'.


Although Cromwell had some disagreements with Sweden and even more with
the Dutch, these two powers did at least share England's Protestantism. But
Cromwell also had to establish relations with the two great Catholic powers
which dominated Western Europe: France and Spain. Throughout the Middle
Ages, the French had been England's main European enemies. By the end of
the sixteenth century, however, England had come to see Spain as her 'natural'
enemy, and was gradually drawing closer to France. Cromwell likewise seems
to have preferred a French alliance, and opened negotiations with Louis XIV's
chief minister, Cardinal Mazarin, early in 1652. Two obstacles soon emerged:
the presence in France of various Royalist exiles, including Charles II; and the
rights of France's Protestant minority. The first was resolved when Louis XIV
agreed to expel the Royalists and give them no more assistance. Discussion of
the second went smoothly until May 1655, when Duke Charles Emmanuel II of
Savoy ruthlessly suppressed a campaign by the Protestants of Piedmont to
preserve their religious freedom. The Duke was a puppet of France, and
French troops were involved in the killing of three hundred Protestants. The
French ambassador in London, Antoine de Bordeaux-Neufville, reported
Cromwell's reaction [5.18].


## 5.18

I have pressed them [ = the English] . . . to sign the treaty . . . But the Secretary of
State [ = John Thurloe] . . . sent me word . . . that his Highness [ = Cromwell]
being moved at the cries and lamentations of the poor Protestants of Savoy, had
resolved first, before he would sign, to send an express to the King [of France] in
[ = on] their behalf; adding many protestations, that it was no pretence to hinder the   5
accommodation [ = alliance], but that the great cruelties which were exercised
against their confraters [ = religious brothers], whereof the news came but today,
and the great authority, which the King hath upon the Duke of Savoy, did oblige
my Lord Protector to do them this office [ = service]; and that he could not sign a
treaty in such a rencounter [ = situation] as this. I confess I was surprised at this   10
alteration, if one do consider the reasons I have for it: first, the advantage this
government will find in the amity [ = friendship] of France; secondly, the assurance
my commissioners gave me of an accommodation; and thirdly, the design of their

fleet in America against the Spanish possessions there [see **5.20–5.23**]. I know not to
what I shall attribute this proceeding, so contrary to all expectation. The zeal of 15
religion certainly is not able to shake the design of the Lord Protector . . . All that I
am able to say is that the sending of this express with a letter to the King doth give
great jealousy [ = suspicion] of mistrust, and that it is a mere pretence, on purpose
to delay the conclusion of the treaty.

**Antoine de Bordeaux-Neufville, French ambassador in England, to the
Comte de Brienne, 24 May 1655, in** *A Collection of the State Papers of John
Thurloe*, **ed. T. Birch, vol. III (London, 1742)**

**5.19** is the text of Cromwell's letter to Louis XIV, dated 25 May 1655.

**5.19**

Most serene King,
The lamentable complaints which have been brought unto us from those poor
distressed people which inhabit, and who profess the reformed religion
[ = Protestantism] in, Lucerna, Angrognia and other valleys [in Piedmont], within
the dominions of the Duke of Savoy, who have of late been most cruelly massacred 5
. . . have drawn these letters from us unto your Majesty, especially seeing we have
also been informed (but how truly, as yet we know not) that this massacre has been
acted partly by some troops of yours, which had joined with other forces belonging
to the Duke of Savoy . . . Now we do not doubt but that your Majesty hath such an
interest and authority with the Duke of Savoy, that by your intercession . . . a peace 10
may very easily be procured for those poor people, with a return into their native
country, and to their former liberty. The performance whereof will be an action
worthy of your Majesty, and answerable to the prudence and example of your most
serene ancestors . . . and will . . . also engage your confederates and allies, which
profess the same religion, in a far greater respect and good affection to your 15
Majesty. As to what concerns us, what favour soever in this kind shall be granted,
either to your own subjects, or shall, by your means, be obtained for the subjects of
others, it shall be no less acceptable to us, yea truly it will be more acceptable, and
valuable, than any other profit and advantage, among those many which we promise
unto our self from the friendship of your Majesty.

**Samuel Morland,** *The History of the Evangelical Churches of the Valleys of
Piedmont*, **book IV (London, 1658)**

After some delay, Louis interceded with the Duke of Savoy, and the religious
rights of Protestants in Piedmont were restored. A further letter from the
French ambassador in London on 23 July 1655 [**5.20**] throws some light both
on French perceptions of Cromwell and on the reasons for Louis's
co-operation.

**5.20**

It seems to me appropriate to be patient in order that the Protector cannot take advantage of this religious zeal which he affects . . . The Protector indeed has the vanity to want to be seen as the defender of the faith, although he does not take the title of it. He flatters himself that our so-called 'reformed' people put all their hope in him . . . Brigadier Stoupe[1] . . . tells me . . . of the intentions of this government,     5
saying that [Cromwell] would rather see war than peace in [Piedmont], and . . . that if his Majesty [the King of France] and . . . the Duke of Savoy do not urge accommodation . . . all the Protestant states and Spain [are] determined, for various reasons, to stir up the conflict.

[1] 'Brigadier Stoupe' = Jean Baptiste Stoupe, a French agent.

Antoine de Bordeaux-Neufville, French ambassador in England, to the Comte de Brienne, 23 July 1655, in F. Guizot, *History of Oliver Cromwell and the English Commonwealth*, trans. A.R. Scoble, vol. II (London, 1854) [my translation]

With the Piedmontese question settled, England and France soon reached agreement and a treaty between them was signed on 24 October 1655.

## Questions

1   What do you make of the phrase 'The zeal of religion certainly is not able to shake the design of the Lord Protector' [**5.18, lines 15–16**]?
2   Would you say that the French suspicions of Cromwell expressed in **5.18** and **5.20** were justified? How?
3   In what ways do **5.18–5.20** provide evidence that Cromwell was a sincere defender of European Protestant minorities?
4   Do **5.18–5.20** show the implementation of ideas outlined in **5.10–5.12**? Explain your answer.

As England's relations with France improved, those with Spain deteriorated. In the later sixteenth and seventeenth centuries, English people hated and feared Spain more than any other European power. They associated Spain with the evils of political tyranny, religious persecution and grandiose imperial ambition. Spain granted Protestants no freedom of worship in her West Indian colonies, and by the early 1650s her constant harrassment of English merchants in the Caribbean had become a serious problem. In the summer of 1654, Cromwell demanded that English merchants in Spanish ports be allowed to worship freely and not be treated as enemies. Spain flatly refused. On 10 July

Cromwell signed a treaty with Spain's enemy Portugal. Ten days later, he proposed that the Council of State launch a military expedition against Spain's colonies in the West Indies. A heated debate followed. **5.21** is an extract from original notes made by one of the Councillors of State, Edward Montague, and records both Cromwell's case in favour of the 'Western Design' and John Lambert's case against it. (For Lambert, see **2.14**.)

**5.21**

[Cromwell:] We cannot have peace with Spain out of conscience to suffer our people to go thither and be idolators. They have denied you commerce unless you be of their religion.

Lambert: 1. The work improbable. 2. Too far off, having greater concernments of settling at home. 3. Not like to advance the Protestant cause, or gain riches to us, or 5 vent [ = an outlet] for troublesome people in England, Ireland or Scotland. 4. The case at first wrong[ly] stated. The charge well considered. The regulation of our law and other concernments not well taken care of it . . .

[Cromwell:] We consider this attempt, because we think God has not brought us hither where we are but to consider the work that we may do in the world as well as 10 at home, and to stay from attempting until you have superfluity [ = a surplus] is to put it off for ever, our expenses being such as will in probability never admit that. Now providence seemed to lead us hither, having 160 ships swimming, most of Europe our enemies except Holland, and that would be well considered also: we think our best consideration had to keep up this reputation and improve it to some 15 good, and not lay them up by the walls. Thence we came to consider the two great crowns [ = France and Spain], and the particular arguments weighed, we found our opportunity point this way. It was told us that this design would cost little more than laying by [ = storing] the ships, and that with hope of great profit.

[Lambert:] Our army in Scotland and army and inhabitants in Ireland must quit the 20 country, or you must find more treasure; or else the West India [ = Western] design must be let fall, and if any of these fall upon us what account shall we give to Parliaments for it?

[Cromwell:] The probability of the good of the design, both for the Protestants' cause and utility to the undertakers, and the cost no more for one twelve month 25 [ = year] than would disband the ships.

*The Clarke Papers: Selections from the Papers of William Clarke,*
ed. C.H. Firth, vol. III (Camden Society, second series, vol. LX, 1899)

The Council supported Cromwell and on 18 August appointed commissioners to plan the 'Western Design'. A fleet was assembled and set sail in December. **5.22** is taken from Cromwell's commission to the commanders of the expedition.

**5.22**

We [ = Cromwell] having taken into serious consideration the state and condition of
the English colonies in . . . America, and the opportunity and means which God
hath betrusted us and this Commonwealth with . . . for securing the interest we
already have in those countries, which now lie open and exposed to the will and
power of the King of Spain (who claims the same by . . . a Donation of the Pope[1]) at    5
any time when he shall have leisure to look that way . . . Whereunto we also hold
ourself obliged in justice to the people of these nations for the cruelties, wrongs and
injuries done and exercised upon them by the Spaniards in those parts. Having a
respect likewise in this . . . undertaking to the miserable thraldom [ = captivity] and
bondage, both spiritual and civil, which the natives and others in the dominions of    10
the said King in America are subjected to . . . by means of the popish and cruel
inquisition and otherwise, from which if it shall please God to make us instrumental
in any measure to deliver them, and . . . to make way for the bringing in . . . of the
Gospel and . . . of true religion and godliness into those parts, we shall esteem it the
best and most glorious part of any success or acquisition it shall please God to bless    15
us with.

[1] 'a Donation of the Pope' = the bull issued in 1493 by Pope Alexander VI dividing lands
discovered in the Americas between Spain and Portugal.

**'The Commission . . . for the West Indian Expedition', 9 December 1654, in**
**The Narrative of General Venables, ed. C.H. Firth (Camden Society, second**
**series, vol. LXI, 1900)**

But the operation went badly wrong. The English troops were poorly trained
and inadequately supplied. An attack on the island of San Domingo in April
1655 was easily defeated, and England's only success was the capture of
Jamaica. Spain was nevertheless furious. A despatch by the Venetian secretary
[5.23] records the reaction of the Spanish ambassador in London.

**5.23**

Since the measures taken here against the Spanish dominion, the Catholic
[ = Spanish] ambassador has rather sought retirement, and is watching rather than
negotiating, greatly indignant at Cromwell's ungrateful and deceitful conduct, upon
which he expressed himself when I saw him recently . . . He said no more except
that he had the same experience as all the other foreign ministers here, namely, that    5
self-interest is the sole guide to the actions of this government. I made no reply
except to say that if instead of going to the Indies the English had sailed to the

Levant[1] in defence of the Christian faith, they would have been loaded with glory, have found an easier task, and possibly a more profitable one.

[1] 'the Levant' = the countries at the east end of the Mediterranean Sea.

**Lorenzo Paulucci, Venetian secretary in England, to Francesco Giustiniani, Venetian ambassador in France, 3 September 1655, in** *Calendar of State Papers Venetian*, **ed. A.B. Hinds, vol. XXX (1655–6)**

On 26 October Spain declared war on England; on 2 April 1656 she agreed to give Charles II substantial help to regain his throne. Meanwhile Cromwell sent a fleet to patrol the Spanish coast so as to prevent aid reaching the West Indies and to intercept the incoming treasure ships on which Spain relied. England successfully attacked Malaga (10 July) and won a naval victory off Cadiz (9 September). But the war proved very expensive, and Cromwell urged Parliament to vote taxes for it. He summarised his view of Spain in his opening speech to the second Protectorate Parliament on 17 September 1656 [5.24].

**5.24**

Why, truly, your great enemy is the Spaniard. He is. He is a natural enemy. He is naturally so; he is naturally so throughout, by reason of that enmity that is in him against whatsoever is of God. Whatsoever is of God, which is in you, or which may be in you, contrary to that . . . [which] his blindness and darkness, led on by superstition, and the implicitness of his faith in submitting to the See of Rome          5
[ = the Papacy], actuate him unto [ = motivate him to do] . . . The Spaniard is your enemy . . . naturally, by that antipathy that is in him and also providentially . . . You could not . . . have an honest nor honourable peace with him. It was sought by the Long Parliament; it was not attained. It could not be attained with honour and honesty . . . [The Spaniard] is naturally throughout an enemy; an enmity is put into   10
him by God . . . And the Spaniard is not only our enemy accidentally, but he is providentially so; God having in His wisdom disposed it so to be, when we made a breach with the Spanish nation, long ago . . . So that a State that you can neither have peace with nor reason from, is that State with whom you have enmity at this time, and against whom you are engaged . . . The plain truth of it is, make any   15
peace with any State that is popish . . . you are bound, and they are loose. Spain hath espoused that interest which you have all along hitherto been conflicting with – Charles Stuart's interest. And I would but meet that gentleman upon a fair discourse that's willing that that person should come back again . . . And truly [Spain] hath an interest in your bowels . . . The papists in England . . . have been   20
accounted, ever since I was born, Spaniolised.

**Cromwell to the second Protectorate Parliament, 17 September 1656, in Carlyle vol. II**

Parliament voted £400,000 for the Spanish war in January 1657. But the conflict was still raging when Cromwell died, and only ended – generally in England's favour – with the Treaty of the Pyrenees (28 October 1659).

## Questions

1  Explain and comment on the following phrases:
   (i) 'the popish and cruel inquisition' [**5.22, lines 11–12**]
   (ii) 'the papists in England . . . have been accounted, ever since I was born, Spaniolised' [**5.24, lines 20–1**].
2  Summarise the cases *for* and *against* the 'Western Design' as laid out in **5.21**. Which do you find the more persuasive, and why?
3  Does **5.22** give a full account of Cromwell's motives for launching the 'Western Design'? Explain your answer.
4  How justified was the Spanish ambassador's reaction, as reported in **5.23**?
5  Comment on the *tone* of **5.24**.
6  Do **5.21**, **5.22** and **5.24** show the implementation of principles set out in **5.10–5.12**? Explain your answer.
7  Would you say that Cromwell pursued the same goals in all three case studies [**5.13–5.17; 5.18–5.20; 5.21–5.24**]? If so, what were they? If not, in what ways were they different?
8  To what extent did Cromwell's relations with European powers constitute 'a Protestant foreign policy'?
9  From the evidence in this chapter, and your wider reading, how successful was Cromwell in achieving his foreign policy aims?

This chapter concludes with three documents [**5.25–5.27**] which criticise Cromwell's foreign policy. **5.25** (like **2.19**) comes from the *Memoirs* of Edmund Ludlow, the former Parliamentarian general who fell out with Cromwell after the dissolution of the Rump Parliament. He wrote his *Memoirs* in exile during the 1660s and 1670s. Document **5.26** (like **2.17** and **4.20**) is an extract from *The World's Mistake in Oliver Cromwell* (1668) by the republican Slingsby Bethel. Finally, **5.27** is taken from a despatch written by the Brandenburg envoy, Johann Friedrich Schlezer, in January 1656. It reports some contemporary attacks on Cromwell and his response to them.

**5.25**

Cromwell, perceiving he could not compass his designs against Spain by his own power, entered into an alliance with the French, who by the treaty with him obliged themselves not to permit the sons of the late King to remain in any part of France; which article was punctually performed. For such is the mystery, or rather knavery of those governments that are framed to support an arbitrary power, that they will     5
not scruple to sacrifice the best friends and nearest relations when they stand in the way of their designs. This confederacy [ = alliance] was dearly purchased on our part, for by it the balance of the two crowns of Spain and France was destroyed, and a foundation laid for the future greatness of the French, to the unspeakable prejudice of all Europe in general, and of this nation in particular, whose interest it     10
had been to that time accounted to maintain that equality as near as might be.

*The Memoirs of Edmund Ludlow*, ed. C.H. Firth, vol. II (Oxford, 1894)

**5.26**

Cromwell began his usurpation upon the greatest advantages imaginable, having it in his power to have made peace, and profitable leagues, in what manner he pleased with our neighbours, every one courting us then, and being ambitious of the friendship of England. But as if the Lord had infatuated, and deprived him of common sense and reason, he neglected all our golden opportunities, misimproved     5
the victory God had given us over the United Netherlands, making peace (without ever striking stroke) so soon as ever things came into his hands, upon equal terms with them. And immediately after, contrary to our interest, made an unjust war with Spain, and an impolitic league with France, bringing the first thereby under, and making the latter too great for Christendom, and by that means broke the     10
balance between the two Crowns of Spain and France, which his predecessors the Long Parliament had always wisely preserved . . . Oliver, instead of advancing the reformed [ = Protestant] interest, hath by an error in his politics been the author of destroying it.

Slingsby Bethel, *The World's Mistake in Oliver Cromwell* (London, 1668)

**5.27**

[Cromwell] told me . . . [that] he knew well enough that he himself must be subject to the opinions of other people, who thought that he used religion and God's name, which, indeed, should be our dearest treasure, only as a pretext, though his deeds would bear witness in the future of the intentions and opinions which he had cherished.

Johann Friedrich Schlezer, envoy of Brandenburg in England, to the Elector Friedrich Wilhelm I of Brandenburg, 11 January 1656, in *Urkunden und Aktenstücke zur Geschichte des Kurfürsten Friedrich Wilhelm von Brandenburg*, vol. VII, ed. B. Erdmannsdörffer (Berlin, 1877) [my translation]

## Questions

1  Are the criticisms of Cromwell's foreign policy expressed in **5.25–5.27** similar or different? Explain your answer.

2  What evidence *for* and *against* the statements in each of **5.25–5.27** have you found in this chapter, and elsewhere?

3  How convincing do you find Cromwell's reply to his critics in **5.27**?

4  Documents **5.25** and **5.26** were both written after 1660 with the benefit of hindsight. Does this affect their validity as attacks on Cromwell's foreign policy?

5  Looking back over the whole of this chapter, would you say that Cromwell pursued similar goals in both his British and his foreign policies? Explain your answer.

6  How can Cromwell's policies towards Scotland, Ireland and Europe be related to any of his other attitudes as revealed in earlier chapters?

7  Discuss and debate the following two assessments of Cromwell:
   (i) 'an imperialist who tried to enhance England's political and economic influence in Britain and the world'
   (ii) 'a religious zealot whose faith determined his policies towards foreign powers'.

# 6 Assessment: historians on Cromwell

So far in this book, we have been looking at seventeenth-century documents: at Cromwell's own letters and speeches, at official ordinances and memoranda, and at the comments and opinions of his contemporaries. This concluding chapter has a rather different purpose. All the documents were written by historians between the late nineteenth century and the present day. They illustrate the very diverse ways in which Cromwell's career has been viewed, and the different reasons why historians admire or condemn him. The ten documents are grouped around three themes. The first four all consider Cromwell's place in English history, the nature of his successes and failures, and the extent to which his achievements died with him. Then follow three extracts focusing on the contradictions within Cromwell's own personality, and the tensions between him and his Parliaments. Finally, there are three extracts which stress Cromwell's sincerity and integrity, and argue that his political actions were motivated primarily by his religious convictions.

Document **6.1**, taken from a set of six lectures by S.R. Gardiner, discusses Cromwell's long-term significance in English history from a late-Victorian perspective. By contrast, **6.2**, written by Christopher Hill at the end of the 1960s, offers alternative reasons why we should remember Cromwell. **6.3** and **6.4**, by Derek Hirst and J.P. Kenyon, are both taken from general surveys of Stuart England but give sharply conflicting accounts of Cromwell's career. Hirst's broadly favourable verdict argues that some of Cromwell's achievements did survive him, whereas Kenyon sees him as an obstacle to settlement, and a betrayer of his own proclaimed ideals.

## 6.1

What may fairly be demanded alike of Cromwell's admirers and of his critics is that they shall fix their eyes upon him as a whole. To one of them he is the champion of liberty and peaceful progress, to another the forcible crusher of free institutions, to a third the defender of oppressed peoples, to a fourth the asserter of his country's right to dominion. Every one of the interpreters has something on which to base his 5 conclusions. All the incongruities of human nature are to be traced somewhere or

other in Cromwell's career. What is more remarkable is that this union of
apparently contradictory forces is precisely that which is to be found in the English
people, and which has made England what she is at the present day . . . With
Cromwell's memory it has fared as with ourselves. Royalists painted him as a devil.     10
Carlyle painted him as the masterful saint who suited his peculiar Valhalla. It is
time for us to regard him as he really was, with all his physical and moral audacity,
with all his tenderness and spiritual yearnings, in the world of action what
Shakespeare was in the world of thought, the greatest because the most typical
Englishman of his time. This, in the most enduring sense, is Cromwell's place in     15
history. He stands there, not to be implicitly followed as a model, but to hold up a
mirror to ourselves, wherein we may see alike our weakness and our strength.

**S.R. Gardiner, *Cromwell's Place in History* (Longman, London, 1897)**


6.2

If we emphasize the 1640s we can with Marvell see Oliver Cromwell as 'the force of
angry heaven's flame', an elemental power cleaving its way through all opposition
'to ruin the great work of time, and cast the kingdom old into another mould'. Or
we can see him as the fiery protagonist of greater liberty of thought and
opportunity, hostile to dogmatism, privilege and shams. If on the other hand we     5
dwell on Cromwell's suppression of the Levellers and his subsequent uneasy career,
he appears an all-too-human class-conscious conservative, a wily politician using all
his arts to preserve a hated military regime – and as the founder of the British
Empire. We can no doubt find threads of continuity in Oliver's personality, his
religion, his social prejudices . . . I sympathise with the ageing, disillusioned man     10
who struggled on under the burden of the protectorate, knowing that without him
worse would befall: who wanted to be painted 'warts and all'. But it is the boisterous
and confident leader of the 1640s who holds my imagination, and whose pungent,
earthy truths echo down the centuries. So long as men and women 'with the root of
the matter in them' call in question those values of their society which deny our     15
common humanity, so long indeed as the great issues of liberty and equality which
Oliver raised remain unresolved, so long will he continue to fascinate, and the
debate over him will continue.

**Christopher Hill, *God's Englishman* (Penguin edition, Harmondsworth, 1972)**


6.3

Not all contemporaries scorned Oliver's achievements. As hostile an observer as
Clarendon could acknowledge that 'brave, bad man', for Cromwell's soldiers and
sailors had made England the most respected military power in Europe. The
contrast with that record was to embarrass Charles II. More generally, Cromwell
had astonished the world and gratified republican political theorists by showing that     5
a strong state could be built, as it seemed, from scratch. Fortified by his belief in
God's providence, he had coped with that doctrine of necessity which had caused

his predecessors, Charles I and the Long Parliament, such unease. He would have impressed those earlier students of fortune and necessity, the Roman Tacitus and the Italian Machiavelli. Oliver of course prided himself on his efforts not only as an   10
Englishman but as a Christian. He had ensured freedom of worship for the godly and brought good men into public life. Others too could praise him, and not merely in retrospect – even in 1656 Richard Baxter could 'bless God for the change that I see in this country'. The rooting of dissent in the previously unevangelized uplands of Wales and the north is one of the most lasting achievements of the Interregnum.

**Derek Hirst,** *Authority and Conflict: England, 1603–1658* **(Edward Arnold, London, 1986)**

**6.4**

Cromwell's character remains very much an enigma, but it is clear that much of the praise lavished on him then and later is misplaced. In the early 1650s he alone stood between the English people and a peaceful and permanent settlement; without his leadership and his military genius, the republic would have foundered in its first two years; single-handed he postponed the inevitable restoration of the monarchy for   5
another ten. Moreover, his increasing authoritarianism so weakened the cause for which he had struggled that after his death his bewildered and demoralised successors had to recall Charles II on his own terms, without imposing on him conditions which would have made the introduction of authoritarian government impossible and the Revolution of 1688 unnecessary. To the end he maintained his   10
dignity, his sense of fairness, and above all his sense of humour; nevertheless, continued military victory, culminating in the 'crowning victory' of Worcester, gave him an undue confidence in the possession of God's peculiar grace – the antinomian pitfall which awaited all Puritans.

**J.P. Kenyon,** *Stuart England* **(Penguin, Harmondsworth, 1985)**

## Questions

1  What are the main reasons presented in **6.1** and **6.2** for studying Cromwell's career? To what extent are they compatible? How persuasive do you find them? Explain your answers.
2  How convincing do you find the arguments advanced in **6.3** and **6.4**? Justify your response.
3  What evidence for and against the arguments advanced in **6.1–6.4** have you encountered in this book, and elsewhere?

The next three extracts [**6.5–6.7**] all analyse Cromwell's career in terms of the deep tensions between him and the Parliaments of the 1650s, and relate these to the contradictions within Cromwell's own personality. In **6.5**, Blair Worden diagnoses Cromwell as an 'ideological schizophrenic', a split personality torn between social conservatism and religious extremism. Worden argues that this was why Cromwell tried hard to work with the Rump Parliament yet ultimately destroyed it. **6.6**, drawn from Austin Woolrych's study of Barebone's Parliament, depicts Cromwell as a ruler pursuing incompatible ideals of religious radicalism and constitutional conservatism. This section concludes with H.R. Trevor-Roper's account of Cromwell's turbulent relations with his Parliaments during the 1650s [**6.7**].

### 6.5

It would . . . be hard to exaggerate the influence of the ambiguities of Cromwell's political temperament on Rump politics. A conservative by social instinct and early political training, he was inspired to spiritual radicalism by his role as God's instrument of victory in the Civil War, by his intimacy with his troops, and by his informal but weighty responsibilities as patron of the religious sects. What resulted     5 was (to simplify) a kind of ideological schizophrenia, setting him on an almost predictable course of political self-destruction. Whenever the social order seemed in peril, whenever the spectre of anarchy was raised, he would expound the virtues of harmony and property and set about repairing the damage; but when he had done so, and when inevitably the cause then strayed once more from the paths of     10 righteousness and reform, he would inveigh against the soullessness of his more temperate colleagues, and destroy the goodwill he had so scrupulously fostered. Endlessly patient in building political unity, Cromwell was sudden and terrible in its destruction. So it was with the Rump government, which he took such pains to create and which he was so dramatically to shatter.

Blair Worden, *The Rump Parliament, 1648–1653* (Cambridge University Press, Cambridge, 1974)

### 6.6

[The readiness of most members of Barebone's Parliament to resign by December 1653] can be explained partly by their awareness that the assembly had no real claim to speak for their communities. But once these communities found their voice again, they reawoke the conflict between radical Puritanism and conservative constitutionalism within the breast of Oliver Cromwell. He did not talk in such     5 abstractions, but he spoke repeatedly of 'the interest of the people of God' on the one hand and 'the interest of this nation' on the other, meaning by the latter the prevailingly traditionalist and secular temper that he found in his Parliaments and in his dealings with the gentry in their counties. It was the need to carry them with

him that made his favourite goals so hard to achieve, but he made it his highest aim     10
to bring the cause of the people of God and the common desires of the political
nation into accord. 'He sings sweetly that sings a song of reconciliation between
these two interests', he said, 'and it is a pitiful fancy and wild and ignorant, to think
they are inconsistent.' His words were far too optimistic, but he did not give up the
attempt to gain the willing assent of MPs and magistrates to measures that would     15
make England worthy of her role as an elect nation. Had he bowed to the worldly
wisdom of frankly pursuing a course of conservative reaction that would have
pleased them better, his path might have been smoother.

**Austin Woolrych, *Commonwealth to Protectorate* (Oxford University Press,
Oxford, 1982)**

### 6.7

On a superficial level, Cromwell was as great an enemy of Parliament as ever
Charles I or Archbishop Laud had been, the only difference being that, as an
enemy, he was more successful: he scattered all his Parliaments and died in his bed,
while theirs deprived them of their power and brought them both ultimately to the
block. Nevertheless, between Cromwell and the Stuarts, in this matter, there was a     5
more fundamental difference than this; for even if he could never control his
Parliaments in fact, Cromwell at least never rejected them in theory. This is not
because he was deliberately consistent with his own parliamentary past. Cromwell
was deliberately consistent in nothing. No political career is so full of undefended
inconsistencies as his. But he was fundamentally and instinctively conservative, and     10
he saw in Parliament part of the natural order of things. He did not regard it, as
Archbishop Laud had regarded it, as 'that hydra' or 'that noise': he regarded it as
the necessary legislature of England; and it was merely, in his own eyes, an
unfortunate and incomprehensible accident that his own particular Parliaments
consistently fell below the traditional standard of usefulness. Therefore again and     15
again he wrestled with the hydra, sought to shout down the noise; and again and
again, like the good man in a tragedy, caught in the trap of his own weakness, he
resorted to force and fraud, to purges, expulsions and recriminations. He descended
like Moses from Sinai upon the naughty children of Israel, smashing in turn the
divine constitutions he had obtained for them; and the surprised and indignant     20
members, scattered before their time, went out from his presence overwhelmed with
turbid oratory, protestations of his own virtue and their waywardness, romantic
reminiscences, proprietary appeals to the Lord, and great broken gobbets from the
Pentateuch and the Psalms.

**H.R. Trevor-Roper, 'Oliver Cromwell and his Parliaments', in his *Religion,
the Reformation and Social Change* (Macmillan, London, 1967), first
published in *Essays Presented to Sir Lewis Namier*, ed. Richard Pares and
A.J.P. Taylor (Macmillan, London, 1956)**

## Questions

1   What evidence for and against Blair Worden's suggestion that Cromwell suffered from 'ideological schizophrenia' [6.5, **line 6**] have you encountered in this book, and elsewhere?

2   (i) 'Cromwell was deliberately consistent in nothing' [6.7, **lines 8–9**].
(ii) 'the good man in a tragedy' [6.7, **line 17**].
Discuss and debate these two statements in H.R. Trevor-Roper's evaluation of Cromwell.

3   Comment on the comparisons which H.R. Trevor-Roper makes between Cromwell and the Stuarts [6.7].

4   Are 6.5–6.7 presenting broadly compatible arguments or conflicting ones? Explain your answer.

5   'Cromwell's difficulties with his Parliaments can only be understood in terms of his own contradictory personality.' Discuss with reference to 6.5– 6.7, and to the evidence which you have found elsewhere in this book.


The final sequence of documents addresses the question of whether Cromwell had any clear and consistent aims or whether he was merely a self-interested pragmatist. In 6.8, Robert S. Paul challenges the view of Cromwell as a hypocrite, and argues that he was fundamentally sincere and principled. 6.9 and 6.10, by C.H. Firth and John Morrill, suggest that the apparent contradictions in Cromwell's political career may be explained in terms of his intense religious convictions, his burning desire to conform to the will of God.


### 6.8

Cromwell became a 'dictator', but it was not from choice. Events had their own way of pushing him to the fore and ultimately to the head of affairs, and the very circumstances of his rise prevented that popular recognition which would have set the seal to his mission. Nevertheless, although only a person 'mistaken and greatly mistaken' would imagine that he consciously schemed for the position which he came to occupy, when the chance of taking the government presented itself he took it firmly. It is within that paradox that what he did sometimes seems to belie what he said. Yet to suggest a fundamental hypocrisy – whether on the grounds advanced by seventeenth century royalists, or on those put forward by twentieth century realists – is to offer a solution too simple to be acceptable. It is too simple because it ignores what is perhaps the most singular fact of Cromwell's career – that throughout the vast accumulation of his uttered thought that has come down to us, never once does he admit a lesser motive in private conversation, public speech, or in his most intimate correspondence. No man could have forwarded his own self-

5

10

interest to achieve a public career of such magnitude without giving some hints of    15
his ambition in word or letter, if personal ambition were the only or even the
predominant motive of the career; and yet few men in history appear to have acted
more consistently and with a clearer conscience than Oliver Cromwell. The
explanation of this can only be that within Cromwell's own mind his ambition was
itself the instrument of a greater cause which he served with absolute sincerity.

**Robert S. Paul,** *The Lord Protector* **(Lutterworth Press, London, 1955)**


**6.9**

Cromwell was a statesman of a different order from most. Religious rather than
political principles guided his action, and his political ideals were the direct outcome
of his creed. Not that purely political considerations exercised no influence on his
policy, but that their influence instead of being paramount was in his case of only
secondary importance . . . Cromwell believed in 'dispensations' rather than    5
'revelations'. Since all things which happened in the world were determined by
God's will, the statesman's problem was to discover the hidden purpose which
underlay events . . . With Cromwell, in every political crisis this attempt to interpret
the meaning of events was part of the mental process which preceded action. As it
was difficult to be sure what that meaning was, he was often slow to make up his    10
mind, preferring to watch events a little longer and to allow them to develop in
order to get more light. This slowness was not the result of indecision, but a
deliberate suspension of judgement. When his mind was made up there was no
hesitation, no looking back; he struck with the same energy in politics as in war.
This system of being guided by events had its dangers. Political inconsistency is    15
generally attributed to dishonesty, and Cromwell's inconsistency was open and
palpable . . . On the other hand, this failure to look far enough ahead, while it
detracts from Cromwell's statesmanship, helps to vindicate his integrity . . . His
system of being guided by events instead of revelations did not put an end to the
possibility of self-deception, though it made it less likely.

**C.H. Firth,** *Oliver Cromwell and the Rule of the Puritans in England* **(Oxford
University Press, Oxford, 1900)**


**6.10**

[Cromwell] was unable to settle for what he had already achieved, a world made safe
for the gentry and the propertied, a prudent measure of religious pluralism, an
effective English imperialism, especially within Britain. He insisted on going beyond
freeing the godly into liberating the ungodly, seeking to turn them from the things
of the flesh to those of the spirit, from carnal reasoning to the responsibilities of    5
Christian freedom, to recognizing and obeying the Will of God. He could not settle
for a vanguard State in which an enlightened minority representing the various
forms of godliness in the nation governed for the unregenerate majority. He wanted

the godly to be the leaven in the lump. He wanted to find a constitutional form that
would either frogmarch (Barebone's/the Major-Generals) or wheedle (the 'healing      10
and settling episodes') God's new elect nation, the English, to the new Promised
Land. He had a vision of building a more just and a less sinful society. A man more
willing to relax with his achievements, to settle for settlement, could probably have
handed on a constitutional monarchy, liberal in its political and religious values, to a
new royal House. But a man with a less fierce vision, with a more compromising        15
spirit, with less certainty of God's special call to him and to England, would never
have risen from being a failed Huntingdon business man and fenland farmer to be
head of state and Lord Protector of a united England, Scotland and Ireland. The
nature of his achievement divided his contemporaries as it divides historians . . .
Cromwell was from the moment of his death one of the best-known and least easily     20
understood of all the great men of history.

**John Morrill, 'Cromwell and his Contemporaries', in** *Oliver Cromwell and*
*the English Revolution,* **ed. John Morrill (Longman, Harlow, 1990)**

## Questions

1   What evidence for and against the views of Cromwell expressed in **6.8–6.10**
    have you found elsewhere in this book, and in your wider reading?
2   Are the ten extracts in this chapter presenting broadly similar images of
    Cromwell or divergent ones? Explain your answer.
3   'The facts of history never come to us "pure" . . . they are always refracted
    through the mind of the recorder . . . When we take up a work of history our
    first concern should not be with the facts which it contains but with the
    historian who wrote it' (E.H. Carr, *What is History?*). Discuss and debate
    with reference to **6.1–6.10**.
4   Using the material in this book, and elsewhere, write your own brief (about
    300 words) assessment of Cromwell's career.

# Bibliography

This Bibliography is divided into two parts. The first contains some general works relating to Cromwell's life and times. It gives details of bibliographies, biographies, surveys, collections of essays and collections of documents. The second part lists some more specialised books and articles which illuminate particular themes. These items are arranged under the relevant chapter heading.

## General works

### Bibliographies

The literature on Oliver Cromwell's life and career is vast. Over 3,500 relevant items are listed in *A Bibliography of Oliver Cromwell: A List of Printed Materials*, ed. W.C. Abbott (Cambridge, Mass., 1929). This may be supplemented by P.H. Hardacre, 'Writings on Oliver Cromwell since 1929', *Journal of Modern History* XXXIII (1961), 1–14.

Details of further useful books and articles published before 1962 are given in the *Bibliography of British History: Stuart Period, 1603–1714*, ed. G. Davies and M.F. Keeler (Oxford, 1970). J.S. Morrill, *Critical Bibliographies in Modern History: Seventeenth Century Britain, 1603–1714* (Folkestone, 1980), discusses 873 books and 478 articles mostly published between 1962 and 1980.

For more recent publications, see the *Royal Historical Society Annual Bibliography of British and Irish History* (Hassocks, annually since 1976), ed. G.R. Elton (1976–85), D.M. Palliser (1986–8), and Barbara English and J.J.N. Palmer (1989– ).

### Biographies

There are innumerable biographies of Cromwell, but that which Dr Blair Worden is currently preparing will surely supersede all of them. In the meantime, the following, listed in alphabetical order, are the most highly recommended:

John Buchan, *Oliver Cromwell* (London, 1934)
C.H. Firth, *Oliver Cromwell and the Rule of the Puritans in England* (Oxford, 1900)
Antonia Fraser, *Cromwell, Our Chief of Men* (London, 1973)
S.R. Gardiner, *Oliver Cromwell* (London, 1899)

Christopher Hill, *God's Englishman* (Penguin edition, Harmondsworth, 1972)
Roger Howell, *Cromwell* (London, 1977)
Robert S. Paul, *The Lord Protector* (London, 1955)

Of these lives, the finest are probably those by Firth, Paul and Hill.

## Surveys

The following surveys all provide background information on English history during Cromwell's lifetime. They are listed in ascending order of complexity, starting with those which assume least prior knowledge:

Austin Woolrych, *England without a King, 1649–1660* (London, 1983)
Toby Barnard, *The English Republic, 1649–1660* (Harlow, 1982)
Barry Coward, *The Stuart Age* (London, 1980)
J.P. Kenyon, *Stuart England* (2nd edition, Harmondsworth, 1985)
Conrad Russell, *The Crisis of Parliaments: English History, 1509–1660* (Oxford, 1971, reprinted 1978)
G.E. Aylmer, *Rebellion or Revolution? England, 1640–1660* (Oxford, 1986)
Derek Hirst, *Authority and Conflict: England, 1603–1658* (London, 1986)

## Collections of essays

The following collections contain many valuable essays on various aspects of Cromwell's life and times:

*The Interregnum*, ed. G.E. Aylmer (London, 1972)
*Cromwell: A Profile*, ed. Ivan Roots (London, 1973)
*Oliver Cromwell and the English Revolution*, ed. John Morrill (Harlow, 1990)

Those essays which are particularly relevant to the themes of this book are mentioned in the appropriate sections below.

## Collections of documents

The most accurate and accessible collection of Cromwell's own letters and speeches, which has been cited throughout this book, is *The Letters and Speeches of Oliver Cromwell, with Elucidations by Thomas Carlyle*, ed. S.C. Lomas (3 vols., London, 1904). This edition also includes an excellent introduction by C.H. Firth. The other main edition of Cromwell's own words is *The Writings and Speeches of Oliver Cromwell*, ed. W.C. Abbott (4 vols., Cambridge, Mass., 1937–47), but although this contains more Cromwell material it is less widely available and is more difficult to use. Twenty-six of Cromwell's most important speeches (plus ten illuminating conversations) have recently been published in a very handy edition: *Speeches of Oliver Cromwell*, ed. Ivan Roots (London, 1989).

Much else about Cromwell may be learnt from ordinances, memoranda and other official documents published during the 1640s and 1650s. For these, the following three collections are especially helpful:

> *The Constitutional Documents of the Puritan Revolution, 1625–1660*, ed. S.R. Gardiner (2nd edition, Oxford, 1899)
> *Acts and Ordinances of the Interregnum, 1642–1660*, ed. C.H. Firth and R.S. Rait (3 vols., London, 1911)
> *The Stuart Constitution*, ed. J.P. Kenyon (2nd edition, Cambridge, 1986)

## Specialised works

### Chapter 1: Cromwell and the Civil Wars

The fullest account of Cromwell's political career during the 1640s is J.S.A. Adamson, 'Oliver Cromwell and the Long Parliament', in *Oliver Cromwell*, ed. Morrill, pp. 49–92.

For an examination of Cromwell's military career in the two Civil Wars, see Austin Woolrych, 'Cromwell as a soldier', in *Oliver Cromwell*, ed. Morrill, pp. 93–118.

Further discussion of Cromwell's role, and of the army's involvement in politics, may be found in:

> Clive Holmes, *The Eastern Association in the English Civil War* (Cambridge, 1974)
> Mark A. Kishlansky, *The Rise of the New Model Army* (Cambridge, 1979)
> Austin Woolrych, *Soldiers and Statesmen: The General Council of the Army and its Debates, 1647–8* (Oxford, 1987)
> David Underdown, *Pride's Purge: Politics in the Puritan Revolution* (Oxford, 1971)

### Chapter 2: Cromwell's political attitudes

There are two complementary surveys of Cromwell's political attitudes in Derek Hirst, 'The Lord Protector, 1653–1658', and Johann Sommerville, 'Oliver Cromwell and English Political Thought', both in *Oliver Cromwell*, ed. Morrill, pp. 119–48 and 234–58.

For Cromwell's relationship with his Parliaments, see H.R. Trevor-Roper, 'Oliver Cromwell and his Parliaments', in his *Religion, the Reformation and Social Change* (London, 1967), pp. 345–91 (reprinted in *Cromwell*, ed. Roots, pp. 91–135).

Studies of Cromwell's handling of particular Parliaments are presented in:

> Blair Worden, *The Rump Parliament, 1648–1653* (Cambridge, 1974)
> Austin Woolrych, *Commonwealth to Protectorate* (Oxford, 1982)

The finest analysis of Cromwell's attitudes towards the kingship remains C.H. Firth, 'Cromwell and the Crown', *English Historical Review* XVII (1902), 429–42, and XVIII (1903), 52–80.

## Chapter 3: Cromwell's religious attitudes

The best introduction to Cromwell's religious attitudes is J.C. Davis, 'Cromwell's Religion', in *Oliver Cromwell*, ed. Morrill, pp. 181–208.

Cromwell's religious development in his early years, and the role of Thomas Beard, are discussed in John Morrill, 'The Making of Oliver Cromwell', in *Oliver Cromwell*, ed. Morrill, pp. 19–48.

Three recent essays by Blair Worden are indispensable for any study of Cromwell's religious beliefs:

> Blair Worden, 'Oliver Cromwell and the Sin of Achan', in *History, Society and the Churches: Essays in Honour of Owen Chadwick*, ed. D. Beales and G. Best (Cambridge, 1985), pp. 125–45
>
> Blair Worden, 'Toleration and the Cromwellian Protectorate', in *Persecution and Toleration: Studies in Church History*, vol. XXI, ed. W.J. Sheils (Oxford, 1984), 199–233
>
> Blair Worden, 'Providence and Politics in Cromwellian England', *Past and Present* CIX (November 1985), 55–99

For useful background on wider religious developments in this period, see Claire Cross, 'The Church in England, 1646–1660', in *The Interregnum*, ed. Aylmer, pp. 99–120; and Claire Cross, *Church and People, 1450–1660* (Hassocks, 1976).

## Chapter 4: Cromwell's social attitudes

The most helpful introductions to Cromwell's social aims are:

> Anthony Fletcher, 'Oliver Cromwell and the Godly Nation', in *Oliver Cromwell*, ed. Morrill, pp. 209–33
>
> Roger Howell, 'Cromwell and English Liberty', in *Freedom and the English Revolution: Essays in History and Literature*, ed. R.C. Richardson and G.M. Ridden (Manchester, 1986), pp. 25–44
>
> Austin Woolrych, 'The Cromwellian Protectorate: A Military Dictatorship?', *History* LXXV (1990), 207–31
>
> Austin Woolrych, 'Oliver Cromwell and the Rule of the Saints', in *Cromwell*, ed. Roots, pp. 50–71

For Cromwell's attempts to realise his aims, see:

> Anthony Fletcher, 'Oliver Cromwell and the Localities: The Problem of Consent', in *Politics and People in Revolutionary England*, ed. Colin Jones *et al.* (Oxford, 1986), pp. 187–204
>
> David Underdown, 'Settlement in the Counties, 1653–1658', in *The Interregnum*, ed. Aylmer, pp. 165–82
>
> J.P. Cooper, 'Social and Economic Policies under the Commonwealth', in *The Interregnum*, ed. Aylmer, pp. 121–42

## Chapter 5: Cromwell and the world

### Britain

The best surveys of Cromwell's British policies are:

> David Stevenson, 'Cromwell, Scotland and Ireland', in *Oliver Cromwell*, ed. Morrill, pp. 149-80
> Ivan Roots, 'Union and Disunion in the British Isles, 1637–1660', in *'Into Another Mould': Aspects of the Interregnum*, ed. Ivan Roots (Exeter, 1981), pp. 5–23

For Cromwell's conquest and rule of Scotland, see F.D. Dow, *Cromwellian Scotland, 1651–1660* (Edinburgh, 1979).
For his treatment of Ireland, the following are especially useful:

> Patrick J. Corish, 'The Cromwellian Conquest, 1649–53' and 'The Cromwellian Regime, 1650–60', both in *A New History of Ireland, Vol. III: Early Modern Ireland, 1534–1691*, ed. T.W. Moody *et al.* (Oxford, 1976), 336–52 and 353–86
> T.C. Barnard, 'Planters and Policies in Cromwellian Ireland', *Past and Present* LXI (November 1973), 31–69
> T.C. Barnard, *Cromwellian Ireland: English Government and Reform in Ireland, 1649–1660* (Oxford, 1975)

For the history of Wales in this period, see G.H. Jenkins, *The Foundations of Modern Wales: Wales, 1642–1780* (Oxford, 1987).

### The world

J.R. Jones, *Britain and the World, 1649–1815* (Brighton, 1980) is a good general introduction.
Cromwell's foreign policy has received less attention than other aspects of his career. The clearest accounts are:

> Roger Crabtree, 'The Idea of a Protestant Foreign Policy', in *Cromwell*, ed. Roots, pp. 160–89
> Menna Prestwich, 'Diplomacy and Trade in the Protectorate', *Journal of Modern History* XXII (1950), 103–21
> Michael Roberts, 'Cromwell and the Baltic', *English Historical Review* LXXVI (1961), 402–46

There is further useful material, especially on the 'Western Design', in:

> Michael Baumber, 'Cromwell's Soldier-Admirals', *History Today* XXXIX (October 1989), 42–7
> Michael Baumber, *General-at-Sea: Robert Blake and the Seventeenth Century Revolution in Naval Warfare* (London, 1989)
> B.S. Capp, *Cromwell's Navy: The Fleet and the English Revolution, 1648–60* (Oxford, 1989)

# Index